T0274030

TWENTY-NINE GOODBYES

Contents

TWENTY-NINE GOODBYES

Introduction

Every translation of a poem is a reinvention of that poem.

When T. S. Eliot proclaimed that Ezra Pound (1885–1972) was the "inventor of Chinese poetry for our time," what he meant was that other translators had invented Chinese poetry in other languages at other times and that Pound had done it for ours. That was about a century ago, and it's hard to overestimate how prophetic those words were. Pound's "invention" has so thoroughly saturated our expectations of what Chinese poetry sounds like that any translation that doesn't sound like Pound doesn't sound like Chinese poetry.

Pound was also at the forefront of inventing English poetry for our time, and for him Chinese poetry was largely a means to that end. When he published his slim volume of translations in 1915 as *Cathay* (the medieval name for a semilegendary China), there was a new poetic movement afoot called Imagism, which sought to cut through the elaborate sentimental rhetoric and stilted rhyming meters of Victorian and Georgian poetry by focusing on *images* and *things* rather than on emotions and abstractions, using direct speech in free verse. Chinese poetry, with its object-laden landscapes, short sentences, and cryptically retiring speakers, seemed ready made for the task. Pound was so keen on reinventing English poetry in this new idiom that he quipped that the ancient poet Qu Yuan 屈原 (340–278 BCE) was an "Imagiste" two millennia before his time.

It still boggles the mind to think that when Pound "invented" Chinese poetry, he couldn't *read* Chinese poetry. What he did was rewrite the translations of others. Most of his inventions were based on cheat sheets he found in the unpublished notebooks of a specialist on Asian art named Ernest Fenollosa, who had received private lessons on Chinese poetry with an expert in Japan named Mori Kainan 森槐南 (1863–1911). Strictly speaking, therefore, Pound's inventions were reinventions of other people's reinventions of Chinese poetry for our time.

Although Du Fu 杜甫 (712–770) is generally considered China's greatest poet, Li Bai 李白 (701–762) is probably the most beloved. (Some scholars use the old pronunciation Li Bo, and there are other spellings such as Li Po, Ly Pé, Li Pek, etc.) He lived during the "Golden Age" of the Tang dynasty and is no less famous in China than is Shakespeare in England. We should all know at least one of his poems.

So, what does Li Bai's poetry sound like in English? Many different things, as we will see. Let's begin with that "invention" for our time.

1

"Taking Leave of a Friend," Ezra Pound

Blue mountains to the north of the walls,
White river winding about them;
Here we must make separation
And go out through a thousand miles of dead grass.

Mind like a floating wide cloud.
Sunset like the parting of old acquaintances
Who bow over their clasped hands at a distance.
Our horses neigh to each other
                as we are departing.

—EZRA POUND (1915)

It was a convention in imperial China (and still is, to a degree) to escort a close friend for some part of their journey, to the next ridge, to the next town, to the next taxi. The vastness of the empire meant that the literati said many farewells, and the "seeing-off poem" 送別詩 became a literary subgenre. Li Bai himself wrote over 150 of them. Often the friend and place are named in the title. But in this one, an unnamed friend is escorted to a spot outside the walls of an unnamed city where they say their final farewell. The deictic, or "pointing," word *here* (line 3) emphasizes the place and time—right here, right now—putting us in the moment.

Neither friend speaks. They bow with clasped hands, just like in the old movies. Their horses speak (if that's the right word for it) instead of the men. We understand the horses are distressed and unhappy. We grasp the inexpressibility of deep human emotion through those nonhuman voices, strange and transcendent.

This is what Pound's invention of Chinese poetry sounds like: spare, vivid, slightly exotic; lyrical and poignant, but not pretty or sentimental. The music comes from assonance and alliteration: no rhyme, no meter.

Pound could have written two identical four-line stanzas, but he breaks that emerging pattern in the last line with a pause in which the observation about the horses neighing to each other hangs in the air for a moment before we understand why, with all its pathos. He uses four sentence fragments, or clauses without active verbs (*Blue mountains, White river, Mind like, Sunset like*). The other two sentences are fairly straightforward (*we must make, Our horses neigh*).

The title suggests the poet is the one departing, not the friend. Or perhaps both are leaving since *we* (line 3) indicates that both *go out through a thousand miles of dead grass*. That's a lot of dead grass. Sounds symbolic. *Blue mountains* sounds a bit funny, but not more than purple mountains' majesty. *White river* evokes shallows, rocks, and a swift current. Although a cautiously skeptical reader might well have doubts about the translation of abstract and symbolic terms—especially when the translator doesn't know the language and is famous for taking poetic liberties—nevertheless, white is white, and blue is blue. Right? We'll have to come back to that.

Still, let's face it, nobody says *we must make separation.* You can hear the Chinese beneath the "calque" or exotically literal translation. The tone wavers between authenticity and a bad fortune cookie. He could have just written: *Here, we must separate.* But that's not what Pound's invention of Chinese poetry sounds like.

Now come the usual poetic tricks: two similes, the first of which is *Mind like a floating wide cloud.* The simplicity is disarming. When Wordsworth wandered lonely as a cloud, he told us he was lonely, but here we perceive the mental state indirectly. It's just that we don't know whose mental state it is. And *wide?* The *cloud* itself is not *wide* but *floating wide.* The oddness sounds precisely exotic, like another calque. But it's not. (The Old English *wíd* means "across a great expanse," as in "far and wide," which Pound certainly knew, this time extracting the exotic from English itself.) There's also a sunset, which is *like* the separation we are witnessing. But the men are now *old acquaintances*—no longer friends—as though something has been lost in translation. Pound's one linguistic sophistication in the poem comes here, where an enjambment straddling the next line specifies that these are not just any old acquaintances but the type who *bow over their clasped hands.* The suggestion is that the poet and friend are doing exactly this, *at a distance* now, but syntactically these *old acquaintances* are merely part of the sunset's extended simile, neither poet nor friend: *their* hands, not "our" hands. Two other hypothetical guys.

And that's good because bowing on horseback is pretty awkward.

Most readers don't stumble over such details on the way to that final moment of equine sublimity. There is no heavy-handed artifice to trip over, since the similes ease our way through the depiction of human pathos by means of nonhuman Nature. The poem sounds perfectly "natural"—except when it sounds slightly "Chinese"—which is also sort of *natural* because it *is* Chinese. Right?

Well, men bowing over clasped hands sure sounds Chinese. And in one manner of speaking it is: Pound's Chinese. That's to say, Pound's invention of Chinese. It's the very opposite of the effusiveness of Pound's conservative contemporaries, such as the hugely popular British poet Rupert Brooke, whom Pound mocked for writing sonnets. In fact, we could say that as a verse form the sonnet stood for everything Pound wanted to blast out of poetry forever: conventional rhyme, conventional meter, conventional rhetoric, conventional sentiments. And yet the original poem was written by Li Bai in the most conventional of verse forms—the *lüshi* 律詩 (pronounced *lew sher*), or "regulated verse poem"—which is as close to a sonnet in Chinese as you can get. Indeed, for that reason, it has been likened to the sonnet from its very first notice by Europeans in the eighteenth century and up to the present day by such sinologists as Achilles Fang, David Hawkes, Arthur Cooper, and David McCraw, among others. It's a form we should all also know as well as Shakespeare's.

Let's hear it reinvented another way.

2

"A Farewell," Herbert Giles

Where blue hills cross the northern sky,
  Beyond the moat which girds the town,
'Twas there we stopped to say Goodbye!
  And one white sail alone dropped down.
Your heart was full of wandering thought;
  For me,—my sun had set indeed;
To wave a last adieu we sought,
  Voiced for us by each whinnying steed!

—HERBERT GILES (1898)

This is what Chinese poetry sounded like before Ezra Pound. It's hard to believe it's the same poem, and in one sense, of course, it's not. But we might envision the original branching into these different versions, both parts of a single ever-growing "poem." Herbert Giles (1845–1935) was a celebrated professor of Chinese at Cambridge University for three decades, whose translations Pound pillaged for a few of his first "reinventions." (But not this one.)

For the nerds, this version is two quatrains of iambic tetrameter with an alternating rhyme scheme. Unlike Pound's, with its enjambment and extra line break, it follows the Chinese poem line by line, but it just doesn't sound like Chinese poetry. I dare say, it all sounds rather English. Bear in mind, of course, that before English writers began to adopt *la mode* of French *vers libre*, this is what English poetry sounded like, so it makes sense that this is how Giles would also write "Chinese" poetry. Lyrics that didn't sound like this didn't sound like poetry. It certainly sounds a lot more like a sonnet than Pound's does.

How else do Giles and Pound differ? Everything is perfectly grammatical in Giles. No sentence fragments. *Where* and *Beyond* tie the first two lines into the third line. Giles's *hills* are smaller than Pound's *mountains* but still *blue*. Pound puts them *north of the walls*. Giles has them *cross* the *northern sky*. Who's right? Somebody's got to be wrong because the *sky* is not a *wall*. If I didn't read Chinese, I'd call *sky* suspicious because something's gotta rhyme with *Goodbye!* (Good god, Giles, the melodrama, get a grip.) A *town* may be too small for battlements, but this one is defended by a *moat*, which is impressive (but no longer white, btw). The tone of *girds* is distractingly biblical-poetical-comical. How can we not think of loins? Giles uses the past tense, which makes the whole scene a reminiscence—*we stopped to say Goodbye!*—whereas Pound stresses the present moment.

And one white sail alone dropped down. Wait, a *white what*? The only thing *white* in Pound is the river. Definitely no sailors. Here, too, they can't both be right. Right? Pound's *thousand miles of dead grass* are now navigable by boat, and a random traveler has sailed out of sight in symbolic anticipation of the friend's departure. No, it must be the sailor friend. Did he sail off on the *moat*? If yes, he'll be circling back around soon. Hey, we'll have another chance to say: *Goodbye!*

Pound's ponderous *Mind like a floating wide cloud* is what Giles gives blandly as *Your heart was filled with wandering thought.* No "cloud" here, but squint hard and you might see the same wine in two bottles. Giles is clearly referring to the friend but gives *heart*, instead of *mind*—and yet it's a *heart* with a *thought*, not a feeling. His *wandering thought* sounds more like ADHD than wanderlust, but we can blame that on the rhyme he *sought*. Rhyme bias. It would be more precise to say *thoughts of wandering*, but that would send the poet squandering, pondering, laundering. *Your heart was filled with thoughts of wandering/ . . . /We waved and there began our maundering.* Yeah, no.

Pound's sunset is *like the parting of old acquaintances*, a simile. But Giles gives Li Bai a deeply personal sunset of his own in a metaphor of decline: *For me—my sun had set indeed.* (No more wandering for *him*.) Indeed. (Despite the *steed*.)

And then they waved *adieu*, as the English say, or at least they *sought* to wave adieu: The action is intended but apparently interrupted by the horses vocalizing what the men were about to express with hand gestures. The pathos of Pound's version lies in its indirectness: *Our horses neigh to each other/as we are departing.* As the Qing poet Qu Fu 屈復 (1668–1745) puts it: "In the *horse(s) crying* at the end of line eight, an overwhelming sorrow is perceptible beyond the words" 八止寫馬鳴, 黯然銷魂, 見於言外. Indeed, this notion of a poetic language that transcends itself—that speaks "beyond the words" 言外—may be the highest ideal in Chinese poetics. Giles, however, spells it all out for us, pathos to bathos: And then, just as we were about to wave *Goodbye!*, our *adieu* was *voiced for us by our whinnying steeds!* (Blimey, the beasts can read minds.)

We all know that *steeds* are grand, studly creatures, but here it sounds tongue-in-cheek, like a poetic exaggeration, not least because they are *whinnying*, which sounds thin and whiny.

From these two translations, it may be hard to see why another commentator, Mei Chengdong 梅成楝 (1776–1844), wrote of this poem: "Among Li Bai's pentasyllabic sonnets, none other from his brush is so astonishing, sweeping away countless human words, rending the sky and falling back again" 青蓮五律無一首不意在筆先,掃盡人千百言,破空而下. Or why the Qianlong emperor (1711–1799) wrote of it: "This is a master craftsman wielding his axe, who sets his own rules and standards" 大匠運斤,自成規矩.

It would be tempting to describe Pound and Giles as opposite ends of a spectrum, but they are more like two axes on a grid. Before turning to others, first let's see where they intersect.

3

送友人 (Seeing Off a Friend)

青 "blue"	山 mountain	橫 go across	北 north	郭 rampart
白 "white"	水 river	繞 go around	東 east	城 city wall

此 this	地 place	一 one	為 make	別 separate
孤 lone	蓬 tumbleweed	萬 10,000	里 mile	征 journey

浮 drift	雲 cloud	遊 travel + 子 son = traveler		意 thought
落 fall	日 sun	故 old + 人 person = dear friend		情 emotion

揮 wave	手 hand	自 from	茲 here	去 go
蕭 蕭 [soughing sounds]		班 divide + 馬 horse = straying horse		鳴 cry

12

The *lüshi* 律詩, or "Chinese sonnet," arose during the Tang dynasty, a time of artistic flourishing not unlike the English Renaissance, but a whole millennium earlier. Its resemblance to the English sonnet is uncanny. Both are strictly metered with rhymes on alternating lines. Both have three distinct parts, one of which is subdivided into two. Both have a turn or twist. And both were originally novelties influenced by the poetry of another language (Italian, Sanskrit) that evolved into the measure of a poet's craft. Both have exquisite exemplars of the form along with innumerable hackneyed attempts that are technically correct but lifeless, labored, or laughable.

The first key to unlocking the Chinese sonnet is recognizing that it is composed in couplets, though translations rarely show this.

The second key is its *parallelism* 對仗, the twin jewels of the form. *Parallelism* means that both lines of a couplet must match grammatically, word for word (noun for noun, verb for verb, and so on). We call the parallelism *semantic* (or *antithetical*) when the matching words also have contrasting meanings within a category. In the first couplet, for example, the same categories of words appear in the same order in both lines, character by character:

(1) an *adjective* for color (blue, white)
(2) a *noun* for a landscape feature (dry mountain, wet river)
(3) a *verb* of movement (straight, curving)
(4) an *adjective* for a cardinal direction (north, east)
(5) a *noun* for a defensive structure (old ramparts, newer walls)

This also happens in the third couplet:

(1) a *verbal adjective* of movement (floating up, falling down)
(2) a *noun* for a heavenly object (cloud, sun)

(3–4) a *2-part compound* for a person (traveler, friend)
(5) a *noun* for an internal state (thoughts, feelings)

Variety within identity. Fearful symmetry. English, of course, has long words and short words, but since every Chinese character is monosyllabic, the alignment is perfect, truly a thing of beauty. Most *words* in classical Chinese are also monosyllabic, but *compounds* composed of two characters sometimes occur in which the whole is greater than the sum of the parts, such as *old + person = dear friend* (not old-timer) and *travel + son = traveler* (not migrant child).

The third key to the Chinese sonnet is the tripartite arrangement of the four couplets, each of which has its own name:

(1) The first, or "head couplet" 首聯, introduces the scene in simple language with no parallelism.
(2–3) The second, or "chin couplet" 頷聯, shifts into the dense syntax of semantic parallelism to evoke emotion through descriptions of the poet's environment, a technique called "the melding of scene and feeling" 情景交融. The third, or "neck couplet" 頸聯, does the same.
(4) The final "tail couplet" 尾聯 shifts back to a personal tone without parallelism, ideally ending with a striking image or a rhetorical question that resonates beyond the final line.

Typically, the nonparallel couplets framing the poem (head and tail) tend to be temporal and unfolding, whereas the parallel couplets at the center (chin and neck) tend to be spatial and static. Thus, there is a familiar rhythm to the reading of a Chinese sonnet: (1) We enter a scene of human life in motion, then (2–3) drop like a white rabbit into a poetic hole where two sets of isolated and balanced but richly suggestive images of the external world float around us, evoking emotional states; then (4) we pop back up into the human world, shaking our floppy ears in wonder at its joys, its sorrows, its inconstant stay.

But don't look for that pattern here, because Li Bai has bent the rules slightly with this sonnet, creating a new rhythm by swapping the first two couplets: (1) straight into the hole, (2) back up for a stroll, (3) down once more, more deeply than before, then (4) up and away. Experienced readers feel these shifts. You can, too.

4

Categorical Comparatives, with Wang Li

Head Couplet

8c 青白	2a 山水	*verb* 橫繞	8a 北東	2b 郭城
"blue"	mountain	cross	north	rampart
"white"	river	round	east	wall

Chin Couplet

7b 此	2a 地	8b 一萬	*verb* 為	*verb* 別征
this	place	one	make	separate
8b 孤	5a 蓬	\<ditto\>	2a 里	\<ditto\>
lone	bush	10,000	mile	travel

Neck Couplet

verb 浮落	1a 雲日	10c–10c 遊子故人	6b 意情
drift(ing)	cloud	traveler	thought
fall(ing)	sun	friend	emotion

Tail Couplet

verb 揮	6a 手	11c 自	7b 茲	*verb* 去鳴
wave	hand	from	here	go
10d–10d 蕭蕭		10c–10c (5b) 班馬		\<ditto\>
[*sough*]	[*sough*]	straying horse		cry

This "translation" identifies the categories used by Tang po-
ets for parallelism, as summarized by the influential linguist
Wang Li 王力 (1900–1986), as follows:

1a. Heaven (天文): 日 (sun), 月 (moon), 風 (wind),
   雨 (rain), 霜 (frost), 露 (dew), 火 (fire), etc.

1b. Time (時令): 日 (day), 月 (month), 年 (year),
   春 (spring), etc.

2a. Earth (地理): 山 (mountain), 江 (river), 冰 (ice),
   石 (stone), 島 (island), 國 (country), 村 (village),
   路 (road), etc.

2b. Buildings (宮室): 樓 (tower), 門 (door), 檻 (banister),
   井 (well), 塔 (pagoda), 瓦 (tile), etc.

3a. Implements (器物): 舟 (boat), 鐘 (bell),
   劍 (sword), 桌 (table), etc.

3b. Clothing and Accessories (衣飾): 帽 (hat),
   扇 (fan), etc.

3c. Food and Drink (飲食)

4a. Cultural Objects (文具): 筆 (brush), 劍 (sword),
   琴 (zither), etc.

4b. Literature (文學)

5a. Flora (草木花果); *5b. Fauna* (鳥獸蟲魚)

6a. The Body (形體); *6b. Humanity* (人事): 愁 (sad),
   閒 (at ease), 笑 (laugh), 言 (speak), 愛 (love),
   醉 (drunk), 行 (walk), etc.

7a. Identities (人倫): 母 (mother), 友 (friend),
   兵 (soldier), 農 (farmer), 王 (king), 仙 (immortal), etc.

7b. Pronomial Adjectives (代名)

8a. Physical Directions (方位): 東 (east), 上 (up), etc.

8b. Numbers (數目): 幾 (few), 獨 (alone), 半 (half), etc.

8c. Colors (顏色): 金 (gold), 玉 (jade), 銀 (silver), etc.

8d. The "Heavenly Stems" and "Earthly Branches" (干支)

9a. Personal names (人名); *9b. Place Names* (地名)

10a. Synonym Compounds (同義連用字);
  10b. Antonym Compounds (反義連用字);
10c. Binomes (連綿字); *10d. Reduplications* (重疊字)
11a. Adverbs (副詞); *11b. Conjunctions* (連介詞);
  11c. Particles (助詞)

These categories are descriptive, not prescriptive, but they help us see what Li Bai has done. Note how the head and neck couplets draw from the same categories. But the chin and tail couplets use different categories for almost every word. Remember, the middle two couplets are supposed to be the lean and mean ones, but a standard variation allows ambitious poets to make the head couplet parallel also, for a run of three parallel couplets in a row (Du Fu was fond of this), followed by a dramatic unspooling of all that wound-up tension in the final couplet. On rare occasions, poets went bonkers with four parallel couplets, but the locked horns of so many paired terms make it hard to move the herd forward.

Wang identifies three types of parallelism: (A) within a single category, which is the strictest; (B) between related categories; and (C) merely grammatical, which is the loosest. Li Bai's chin couplet appears to belong to type C, which means that the poem actually follows the standard variation: characters #1 and #2 are a *modifier* plus a *noun*: *this place* and *lone bush*; #3 is a number: *once* and *ten thousand*; #4 is tricky because *wei* 為 (make) is an *auxiliary verb* and *li* 里 (mile) is a *measure word*, but both of these could be classified as "empty words" 虛字, as opposed to "content words" 實字; and #5 is a verb: *bie* 別 (separate) and *zheng* 征 (travel). The poem thus conforms to the rules, yet the chin couplet is so loose that we perceive a shifting rhythm. This is what impressed the Qianlong emperor: "The head couplet is well ordered, then the continuation [chin couplet] flows along, and the neck couplet is vigorous and strong. The ending gives the sadness of separation with a delicate touch" 首聯整齊, 承則流走, 而下頸聯健勁, 結有蕭散之致. Qianlong's description of the chin couplet as "flowing along" 流走 is particularly apt because we call the sort of loose pairing of terms in that couplet "flowing water parallelism" 流水對.

5

"Sending Off (a) Friend(s)"

A/*the* "blue" mountain(s) go(es) across a/*the*
   norther*n* rampart(s).
A/*the* "white" river(s) go(es) around *the* eastern
   city wall(s).

At this place, once *you/we* complete *your/our*
   parting,
You/we will be (*a*) lone tumbleweed(s) *that for*
   ten thousand miles journey(s).

A/*the/that/those* drifting cloud(s) *is/are* (*like*)
   a/*the* traveler('s/s') thought(s).
A/*the/that* setting sun *is* (*like*) a/*the/this* dear
   friend('s/s') feeling(s).

You/I/we wave *your/my/our* hand(s) *as*—from
   here—*you/I/we* depart;
With (*a*) soughing sound(s), *your/our/my* straying
   horse(s) cry/cries.

For this odd translation, I've added words in italics as necessary to make complete English sentences. It's almost unreadable like this, I know, but it highlights the grammatical ambiguities in the poem.

Chinese is what linguists call an "isolating" language, which means that the characters (and the spoken words represented by those characters) never ever change from sentence to sentence. Thus, we can't know whether *shan* 山 refers to a single mountain or to many mountains. If you need to be more precise, you can add more words—for example, "many" + *shan* = "many mountains"—but you can't alter *shan*. The verbs never change either, so *heng* 橫 (go across) isn't conjugated as singular or plural; it's both. Articles and most prepositions are optional in classical Chinese, so they also provide none of the typical clues. In line 5, for example, are the thoughts of *a* traveler (like) *a* drifting cloud in general? Or, is the thought of *this* traveler (like) *that* drifting cloud in particular? If you can think like a Tang poet, such distinctions don't matter. You can chill already. Translators, however, rarely have that luxury.

Chinese can also drop its pronouns, which means we don't always know exactly who or what the subject of an action is. In most such "pronoun-drop" languages, the conjugation of the verb encodes the missing pronoun: *andiamo*, for example, tells us who's going out for pizza without the redundant *noi* (*we* are). But since the verbs never change in Chinese, *qu* 去 could mean: *I go, you go, he goes, she goes, we go, absolutely anything goes*. The same is true for tense. The same word *qu* 去 could mean: *I go, we went, they will go*. We must infer *who, what,* and *when* from context and convention or from additional words.

Thus, the two verbs in the penultimate line—"wave" 揮 and "go" 去—allow for seven grammatical permutations just for the present tense: *You wave and you go; I wave and I go;*

you wave and I go; I wave and you go; we wave and you go; we wave and I go; and finally *we wave and we go.* (If you ignore the convention of a direct address to an individual friend, you could even add *he* and *they* into the mix, or *she* for that matter, but grammatical possibility is not the same as probability.) Classical Chinese also often dispenses with possessive pronouns, so we can't be sure whose horse neighs in the final line: *your horse, my horse,* or *our horses.* When combined with the seven permutations above, these three possibilities afford twenty-one different scenarios (*many* more if we include the unlikely third-person pronouns). Translators often just choose whatever sounds best to them.

Some like to make a big deal about how the lack of pronouns in classical Chinese creates an egoless melding of poetic subjectivity with Nature by effacing the presence of a human observer, which is sometimes thought to be intentionally Buddhist or Daoist in effect. True enough. But pronouns are typically *implied* in pronoun-drop languages, and we should not underestimate the power of reading practices to indicate them, aside from the sort of lexically *explicit* terms any student could look up in a dictionary. In other words, in the absence of other contextual clues, the poetic "I" is understood for any active verb lacking a subject in classical verse. In Wang Wei's famous "Deer Park" 鹿柴, for example, the first line reads:

空 empty | 山 mountain | 不 not | 見 see | 人 people

On the empty mountain, I don't see anyone. No experienced reader of Chinese would fail to insert the mind's "I" in this line. There is surely an important difference between *implicit* and *explicit* content in any poem, and one could use the passive voice here to try to mark that difference ("On the empty mountain, no one can be seen"), but the fact remains that a first-person speaker is assumed in the absence of a pronoun in literally thousands of similar Tang poems.

In our poem, however, the presence of two people (and two horses) complicates this convention and preserves a thematically rich grammatical ambiguity that blurs the distinction between speaker and friend as they draw apart. And yet, since the friend is the one who *departs* in a seeing-off poem, one could argue that "*you* depart" is the only option and that *I* and *we* are off the table, thus narrowing twenty-one probable scenarios to nine. On the other hand, one could argue that the place of separation is remote enough that the poet must also depart from it to return home, putting *I* and *we* back on the table. The beauty of this ambiguity is precisely that it fuses the two friends indistinguishably together at the moment they must separate. If one waves, they both do. The disjointed syntax of much modern poetry has taught us how to accept such ambiguity, but translators have traditionally felt the need to add words to make graceful and grammatical sentences. Where should we draw the line? How much invention is allowed in reinvention?

6

"Le départ d'un ami," Judith Gautier

Par la verte montagne aux rudes chemins, je
   vous reconduis jusqu'à l'enceinte du Nord.
L'eau écumante roule autour des murs, et se
   perd vers l'orient.
C'est à cet endroit que nous nous séparons . . .
Je m'en retourne, solitaire, et je marche pénible-
   ment. Il me semble maintenant que j'ai plus
   de dix mille *lis* à parcourir.

Les nuages légers flânent, paresseusement,
   comme mes pensées.
Bientôt le soleil se couche, et je sens, plus vive-
   ment encore, la tristesse de la séparation.
Par-dessus les broussailles, une dernière fois,
   j'agite la main, au moment où vous allez
   disparaître.
D'un long hennissement, mon cheval cherche
   à rappeler le vôtre . . . Mais c'est un chant
   d'oiseau qui lui répond! . . .

—JUDITH GAUTIER (1901)

The Departure of a Friend

By the green mountain with rough roads, I
    escort you all the way to the northern rampart.
The frothing water flows around the walls and
    disappears towards the east.
It is at this place that we will separate . . .
I turn away from it, alone, and I walk painfully.
    It seems to me that I have more than ten
    thousand *li* to travel.

The light clouds roam, lazily, like my thoughts.
Soon the sun sets, and I feel, more strongly than
    before, the sadness of separation.
Over the scrub brush, one last time, I wave my
    hand, at the moment that you are about to
    disappear.
With a long whinny, my horse tries to call yours . . .
    But it is the song of a bird that responds to
    him! . . .

If Ezra Pound was the inventor of Chinese poetry for our time, Judith Gautier (1845–1917) was the inventor for hers. A daughter of the great Parnassian poet and literary critic Théophile Gautier, Judith began studying Chinese at the age of seventeen in 1863 with a Christian convert named Ding Dunling 丁敦齡, who was down and out in Paris at the time. Within a few months, she began publishing imitations (*variations sur des thèmes Chinois*, she called them), and then, as her Chinese improved, free adaptations from other translators, and eventually loose translations of her own. Gautier's reinventions were so popular they were imitated and retranslated into multiple languages, giving a vast number of readers for many years the impression that Chinese poets had a flair for the Romantic and wrote *petits poèmes en prose* like Charles Baudelaire.

Gautier seems to inhabit the poem and reinvent it from the inside out, expressing the poet's emotions openly and explicitly: He returns homeward in such pain he himself becomes the wandering traveler. No longer solitary, the *clouds* become *light* and *roam lazily* (simile alert) *like* his *thoughts*. When the sun sets, he begins to *feel more strongly than before the sadness of separation*, heart on his billowing sleeve. Then the landscape rises again before our eyes with *scrub brush*, over which he must wave, as if the tumbleweed cut from line 4 (Pound's *dead grass*, Giles's *one white sail*) has rolled down into line 7.

Gautier's final line is a bolt out of the sky. Recall that the Chinese doesn't tell us whether it's the poet's horse who neighs, the friend's horse, or both. In Pound and Giles, it's both. But in Gautier the poet's horse alone calls out, in vain, since the other is too far away, about to disappear from sight. Then, a bird, out of the blue.

There are two words for horse sounds in the last line of the original. One is *xiao-xiao* 蕭蕭 (pronounced now like *shee-ow shee-ow*), originally an onomatopoeic term for the swishing or whistling sound made by the wind in the trees and later by horses. As an imitation of the sound, the word probably evoked the way horses sough, or blow out their lips. (Actually, *neigh* and *whinny* are onomatopoeic words, too, but we tend to forget that. So is *hennissement*.) The other word is *ming* 鳴, a general verb for the crying out of animals, birds, or insects. When people *ming*, they tend to be wailing in grief. Millennia ago, the word referred specifically to the cry of a bird, as the composite form of its character demonstrates:

口 (mouth) + 鳥 (bird) = 鳴 (birdcry)

The meaning and pronunciation evolved over time, but the character remained the same. When Gautier looked at the word Li Bai used to name what the horses are doing, what she saw was the poetry of etymology: a bird and a mouth transmuted into the lyrical intangibility of birdsong and the startling loss of a companion. Synthesis, montage, alchemy. This is but one of various ways Chinese characters are formed, comprising only 12% of the total but consuming 100% of the imagination of non-Chinese poets, for obvious reasons. It's like a little poem condensed into a sign. The invisible born of the visible. To expand the etymology of a single word into a whole new line has the sinological authority of a magpie pecking through a dictionary. But what an ending! The protodeconstructive energy is electrifying. It's the best line in Gautier's poem.

7

"Saying Good-Bye to a Friend," Amy Lowell and Florence Ayscough

Clear green hills at a right angle to the North wall,
White water winding to the East of the city.
Here is the place where we must part.
The lonely water-plants go ten thousand *li*;
The floating clouds wander everywhither as does man.
Day is departing—it and my friend.
Our hands separate. Now he is going.
"Hsiao, hsiao," the horse neighs.
He neighs again, "Hsiao, hsiao."

    —AMY LOWELL AND FLORENCE AYSCOUGH (1921)

The siren song of Sino-etymology that inspired the poetic madness of Judith Gautier's bird talking to a horse also seduced Ezra Pound, with results similarly bizarre and sublime. When he posthumously edited Ernest Fenollosa's *The Chinese Written Character as a Medium for Poetry*, he had already begun pecking through a dictionary himself to illuminate the fundamental poetic wisdom of expressing abstract ideas by combining images of concrete things. His attempts were mostly bird-brained from an etymological perspective, but he was sometimes right. Of course, from a poetic perspective, the quality of the poetry itself is the only measure of what's right. So there.

Nobody else articulated that Sino-etymological frenzy more fervently than Amy Lowell (1874–1925) and Florence Ayscough (1875–1942), who vied with Pound to get the scoop on how there were richly significant "overtones" and "undercurrents" in the composition of every Chinese character that had escaped the notice of previous translators. Lowell was the bold American face of the imagist movement; Ayscough was a Canadian-American born in Shanghai. According to the latter, "it is often impossible to seize a poet's complete meaning unless the characters are broken into their component parts." (Phantasm alert: Chinese poetry is no more etymological than English poetry.) She called such translations "split-ups." (Pound called it the "ideogrammic" method.) But despite their fervor for the (creative, experimental, phantasmatic) theory, Lowell and Ayscough were cautious in practice, and they split up characters into phrases only about "a baker's dozen" times, by their own count, in their book of one hundred and twenty poems. Bit of a letdown, if you ask me.

Clear green hills. So far, we've seen *blue* mountains (in Pound) and *green* ones (in Giles) and one *verte* (*chez* Gautier). The word in question is *qing* 青, which refers to a spectrum of

colors from green to bluish green to greenish blue to azure to
black. It's a notorious chromonym, described by one scholar
as "the color of nature," hard to pin down exactly. The Green
Mountains where I live in Vermont are eponymously green,
but they look bluish right now at a distance, greenish blue, in
fact. So there. But why *clear*? Well, Lowell couldn't read any
more Chinese than Pound could, so she relied on crib sheets
prepared for her by Ayscough. Since the following line begins
with the phrase *baishui* 白水 (white water), the first word of
which also means "clear" (we'll come back to this), I'd wager
that Ayscough wrote "clear" above the "white" in her crib as a
second thought, and Lowell cluelessly added it to *green hills*
in the line above. *Sigh.*

How the mountains might *heng* 横 (go across) the north-
ern rampart in the original may be hard to picture, but it
seems they stretch out beyond it, whereas the geometry of *at
a right angle* protrudes from a dictionary (*heng* 横 also means
"horizontal"). The *peng* 蓬 is a plant that dries up and rolls
away in the wind, but if you call it a "tumbleweed," Li Bai
becomes a cowboy with a sidekick. Their lyrical solution
here is *water-plants* floating away instead. *Gu* 孤 (alone) sug-
gests loneliness, yet these collective *water-plants* are *lonely*
even in their tour group. They are mistakenly paired with
floating clouds—which ought to parallel the setting sun—
which itself has vanished into "day" (another meaning of
ri 日 "sun") as *Day is departing*. There are no "feelings" or
"thoughts" but only portentous afterthoughts: *as does man*.
But they penetrate *everywhither*. For all her modernism,
Lowell has one foot in the Victorian era.

No hands clasped in Mandarin flections here or even
waving but only *hands* that *separate*. The dictionary knows
why. The verb *hui* 揮 (wave) also means "scatter," as in the
motion of manually sowing seeds (thus, also "disperse,"
"separate"), but when combined with a *shou* 手 (hand), the

phrase means—wait for it—"wave a hand." My frenemy, the dictionary. Here, it's all about calling the game play by play: (Action 1) *Our hands separate.* (Action 2) *Now he is going.* Lowell and Ayscough place us in the unfolding moment of separation, but the poet seems to be talking to someone else. Yes, *zi* 兹 can mean *now* as well as "here," but the original poem stresses the place, as does the dropped word *zi* 自 (from): the friend departs *from* "here," not *from* "now," though ideally the here-and-now of space-time would not be split apart.

"Hsiao, hsiao," the horse neighs. Lowell and Ayscough are the first to render the onomatopoeic words for horse sounds—assuming the horses speak modern Mandarin and use the Wade-Giles romanization system. (Yes, that Giles.) And *again*, twice. And yet the would-be poignancy seems to land in the lap of Mother Goose. Bow wow, the dog barks. It's not clear whose is *the horse* (singular) doing all the horseplaining (context vaguely implies it's the friend's), but this much we know: *He* is a stallion, does all the talking, and repeats himself portentously, *as does man.*

8

"Adieu," W. J. B. Fletcher

Athwart the northern gate the green hills swell.
   White water round the eastern city flows.
When once we here have bade a long farewell,
   Your lone sail struggling up the current goes.

Those floating clouds are like the wanderer's heart.
   Yon sinking sun recalls departed days.
Your hand waves us adieu; and lo! you start,
   And dismally your horse retiring neighs.

—W. J. B. FLETCHER (1919)

William John Bainbrigge Fletcher (1879–1933) came of age in the last two decades of Queen Victoria's reign, then served as a British consular officer in China, and it shows. His poems are skillful, accurate, and sprinkled with scholarly notes, but lo! with what difficulty he bade farewell to yon sinking Victorian aesthetics.

Fletcher printed the Chinese text with each poem, so we have proof that, unlike Gautier adding her own words (*paresseusement, péniblement*), Fletcher wasn't imagining things when a *sail* entered his translation. It's right there in the Chinese, the second character in the line: 孤蓬萬里征. Note the difference between *peng* 蓬 and *peng* 篷:

逢	+	⁺⁺ (grass)	=	蓬 (tumbleweed)
逢	+	⁀⁀ (bamboo)	=	篷 (sail)

At some point during the long history of reprinting Li Bai's poem, somebody changed the top of the character from *grass* to *bamboo*. I'm guessing the culprit was probably Cao Xuequan 曹學佺 (1574–1647) in an anthology from the early seventeenth century. Modern editors generally reject *peng* 篷 (sail) as a spurious variant, but many readers clearly accepted it as good poetry and kept repeating it, so that in some sense there are now two Chinese "originals" for this poem—one comparing the traveler to a tumbling bush, the other to a sailing vessel. Giles and Fletcher just happened to be reading the latter.

Unlike the ideographic synthesis of *mouth* 口 and *bird* 鳥 into ancient *birdsong* 鳴, which appeals only to the eye, these characters are ideophonetic combinations that appeal to the eye to help the ear, as if to say: this *peng* 蓬 is the *peng* that has to do with *grass* ⁺⁺ (tumbling away), not the *peng* 篷 that has to do with *bamboo* ⁀⁀ (woven into sails), or the *peng* 澎 that has to do with *water* 氵 (the Peng River), or the *peng* 塳 that has to do with *earth* 土 (dust in the wind),

etc. The vast majority of Chinese characters work like this.
A language with monosyllabic words has a lot of homonyms,
after all, so it helps to have ways of distinguishing them
such as tonal inflections, disyllabic compounds, and these
ideational markers called "radicals" 部首. The phonetic
markers in characters are themselves common characters
borrowed for their well-known sound. In *peng* 蓬 (tumble-
weed), the phonetic marker is *feng* 逢 (meet). Their sounds
have diverged in the last millennium, but in Li Bai's day, *peng*
and *feng* were both pronounced *bung*. What's more, *feng* 逢
(meet) itself is composed of the semantic *chuo* 辶 (walk) and
the phonetic *feng* 夆 (oppose, encounter)—once also voiced
as *bung*—which is itself composed of *zhi* 夂 (walk) and the
phonetic *feng* 丰 (lush growth). Ideogrammatize that, Ezra.

Fletcher's *hills* are *green*, which seems salubrious, but
they *swell athwart*, which can't be good. There must be a
tonic for that. Like everyone else, he's struggling to imagine
exactly what those mountains are doing in relation to the
city ramparts. And why *gate* for *guo* 郭 (rampart)? He doesn't
need a variety of diction for *wall*, since, like Lowell and Ay-
scough, he chooses to translate *cheng* 城 as *city* instead of
wall. It could be either. In fact, the word means both *wall*
and *city*, since the urban space is defined by the enclosure,
both physically and metonymically.

Fletcher's *Those* and *Yon* make it clear that the friends ac-
tually see the *floating clouds* and the *sinking sun* that reflect
their internal states (first with a simile, then a recollection).
In the Chinese, the traveler's "thoughts" 意 are parallel with
the poet's own "feelings" 情, balancing head and heart, yet
Fletcher turns "thoughts" into *heart* and "feelings" into *de-
parted days*. But what days? Days of yore? Days of youth?
(He needs a rhyme for *neighs*.) If *qing* 情 (feelings) looks
familiar, that's because it uses *qing* 青 (blue/green) as its
phonetic marker, to which is added *xin* 忄 (heart). Feeling

blue? Feeling green? (It ain't easy, I know.) Then *lo! you start*. So did I, if the truth be told. But the jolt nicely shifts us from stasis to the action of departure. In the end, one horse neighs *dismally*. Fletcher sees the implicit melancholy in the nonhuman sigh but just can't leave it there, so the adverb is added to the verb with all the affective refinement of a salt lick. And yet the same sense of clarity also results in a logical distribution of pronouns: After *we* finish our farewells in line 3, *your* boat will depart in line 4; *your* hand waves, and *you* start (*lo!*) in line 7; then *your* horse neighs (*dismally*, oh, so *dismally*) in line 8. These choices leave the poet passive, motionless, and speechless as the friend departs on horseback toward the moorage at the riverbank (moatbank?) to sail into the sunset.

9

"Valedicit amico," Angelo Zottoli

青	山	橫	北	郭
Viridans	mons	opponitur	boreali	suburbio,

白	水	繞	東	城
limpida*que*	aqua	cingit	orientalem	urbem;

此	地	一	為	別
hic	loci	semel	facto	dissidio,

孤	蓬	萬	里	征
solitaria	conyza*	decemmile	stadia	perget:

浮	雲	遊	子	意
fluitans	nubes	*peregrinantem*	*dominum*	[*repræsentat*,]

落	日	故	人	情
occidens	sol	*amici*	*hominis*	affectum;*

揮	手	自	茲	去
gestu	manùs	ex	loco	dissidentibus,

蕭	蕭	斑	馬	鳴
stridula	*voce*	distracti	equi	hinniunt.*

* Conyza, quæ maturius arescit, et a vento facile difflatur, peregrinantis est imago.

* Suum affectum ad occidentem solem refert, quem frustra respicere voles.

* Non homines modo, sed et ipsi nostri equi longæ consuetudini assueti, ad dissidium dolentes hinniunt. Gestu manûs, quo vale dicitur.

—ANGELO ZOTTOLI (1882)

He Says Farewell to a Friend

The green mountain is opposed by the northern suburb, and the clear water surrounds the eastern city. In this place, once separation is done, the solitary fleabane* will go forth for ten thousand furlongs. A floating cloud represents the wandering master, the falling sun the emotion* of a friendly person. With a gesture of the hand, divided from this place, the separated horses whinny* with a shrill voice.

*   *Fleabane*, which dries up when older and is easily blown about by the wind, is the image of wandering.
*   Connects his emotion to the setting sun, which you will wish in vain to see again.
*   Not only humankind, but also our horses long accustomed to our habits whinny at the painful separation. *With a gesture of the hand*, with which he says farewell.

Angelo Zottoli (1826–1902) was a Neapolitan who lived in China from the age of twenty-two, one in a long line of Jesuit sinologues dating back to the sixteenth century. He passed the imperial examination—a truly impressive feat—and wrote multiple works in Chinese, including a dictionary and a magnum textbook (four thousand pages in five tomes) with translations of all the major Chinese classics into Latin. Giles is reported to have consulted them.

Recall that classical Chinese is an isolating language with a high degree of grammatical ambiguity. Latin, however, is about as far from that as you can get, as an "inflected" language in which the relationships between words are strictly defined by customizable endings ("inflections"). But Latin, like the hedgehog in the old proverb, knows one big trick: It can rearrange the words of a sentence into almost any order and keep the same meaning, all because of those inflections. Pretty foxy, eh? Thus, when Zottoli's prose translation is interlineated with the Chinese it matches almost perfectly. No other language in this book can do this.

In another cool trick, Zottoli attaches -*que* (and) as an "enclitic" to *limpida* (clear), thus connecting the first two lines without adding an extra word, which would spoil the word-for-word matching. He also keeps the word count by rendering the horses' onomatopoeic *xiao-xiao* with the two-word *stridula voce* (shrill voice). And he cleverly translates *youzi* 遊子 (traveler) and *guren* 故人 (friend) to convey both the individual characters as well as their compound meanings. Surely, *amici hominis* (friendly person) is more awkward than *amici* (friend) alone, but it keeps the count. If *amici* feels like a stretch for *gu* 故 (old), that's because we don't normally dissolve compounds—a "butterfly" is not a *fly* of *butter*, though perhaps it was once—but the logic of an "old" relationship leading to "friendly feeling" is not hard to fathom, and a more literal "*veteris* amici" (*old* friend) would have the same tradeoff, since *ren* 人 is just "person," not "friend." Get it?

Zottoli's whopper is to use the verb *repræsentat* (represents) for the noun *yi* 意 (thoughts), which spoils the parallelism with *qing* 情 (feelings). Apparently uncomfortable with the parataxis (i.e., pure juxtaposition) of "floating cloud" and "traveling-person thoughts," he construes *yi* 意 (thoughts) as "conveying the thought of." The flexible word order allows him to put the verb at the end of the clause, which sounds grand in Latin, and since it also governs the next line, he can include the noun this time (情 emotion, *affectum*). Yet despite the flexibility of Latin, Zottoli would rather have a matching word count than recreate the parallelism of one of the most celebrated parallel couplets in Tang poetry. Why not just add *repræsentat* or some other verb to both lines instead of wrenching *yi* 意 (thoughts) into a verb? Parallelism don't get no respect.

10

"Geleit," Alfred Forke

Dort, wo die Stadt die Berge grün
  Von Norden her umschliessen,
Und an der Oststadtmauer hin
  Die weissen Wasser fliessen,

Dort vor dem Thore ist der Ort,
  Wo unser Weg sich scheidet.
Du schweifst in weite Fernen fort,
  Von nun an unbegleitet.

Dein Sinn leicht wie die Wolke scheint,
  Da dir die Ferne winket,
Dieweil daheim das Herz dem Freund'
  Gleichwie die Sonne sinket.

Ein Händedruck noch, mein Genoss,
  Eh' wir uns trennen müssen!
Mit lautem Wiehern scheint dein Ross
  Zum Abschied mich zu grüssen.

—ALFRED FORKE (1899)

Escort

There, where the green mountains
    Enclose the town on the north,
And towards the city wall to the east,
    The white water flows,

There outside the gate is the place
    Where our paths diverge.
You wander away into the vast distance,
    From now on unaccompanied.

Your mind seems light as a cloud
    As the distance beckons you,
With the heart of your friend at home
    Just like the sinking of the sun.

One handclasp more, my friend,
    Ere we must part!
With a loud whinny your steed seems
    To bid me farewell.

Alfred Forke (1867–1944) served as an interpreter in Beijing
for over a decade before working as a professor in Berlin
for over three. Like Giles, his diction now at times feels
fusty, the verse stiff, and the jaunty rhymes at odds with the
sentiments.

It's sometimes tempting to associate specific aesthetic
forms with specific political sensibilities, but of course
there's no essential connection between the two. To say that
if Forke wrote in strict meters, then he musta been a goddam
Nazi would be silly, even though three decades later in 1933
he did sign the teachers' pledge of loyalty to Adolf Hitler
(*Bekenntnis der Professoren an den deutschen Universitäten
und Hochschulen zu Adolf Hitler*) in order to safeguard his
university position. So, he really was a goddam Nazi, but
not because he rhymed his poems. Ezra Pound, who did as
much as any other single poet to blast apart conservative aes-
thetics in the modern era, was a Fascist sympathizer in Italy
in the early 1940s, and the loathsome antisemitism of his
notorious radio broadcasts appears alongside his innovative
poetics in *The Cantos*. How we judge the ostensibly apoliti-
cal art of translations like these by bad political actors is an
enduring quandary for us all. It's hard not to see it as tainted.

Like everyone else, Forke fails to convey the parallelism
in the original. He does, however, isolate the original cou-
plets, each into a quatrain of its own, but then makes the
first one spill over into the second, which he cuts in half,
right in the middle of a sentence. He connects the overflow
with another *Dort* (There): *Dort . . . ist der Ort* (There is the
place). Why *Dort* is the *Ort*, and not *Hier* (Here), is puz-
zling because they seem to be in the here-and-now of the
present. Sound trumps sense. Forke even locates the place
more specifically than the original with *vor dem Thore* (out-
side the city gate) and uses the present tense *Du schweifst
in weite Fernen fort* (You wander away into the far distance),

which lets us watch the action as it happens. The problem with wandering off here is that the friend will have to gallop back again at the end for that *Ein Händedruck noch* (one last handshake).

The tumble-sail crux has vanished into the wind. That was easy. The friend's *Sinn* (mind) is as *leicht* (light, carefree) as a cloud because the far distance beckons to him (Vanderluster that he is), while the *Herz dem Freund* (heart of the friend) is *Gleichwie* (just like) the sinking sun because it remains *daheim* (at home). There you have it, a perfectly logical explanation for a perplexingly paratactic parallel couplet. Forke adds an intimate *mein Genosse* at the end, which wavers between "comrade" and "companion." Could a thirty-year-old Forke have been swayed by the socialist SPD before Hitler got to him three decades later? (That one I leave to the historians.) The friend's horse makes a *lautem Wiehern* (loud whinny), raising the volume on *xiao-xiao*, which only *scheint* (seems) to bid him *Abschied* (farewell), because, of course, horses can't speak. (Did I mention that?) That would be absurd.

11

"Taking Leave of a Friend," Obata Shigeyoshi

Blue mountains lie beyond the north wall;
Round the city's eastern side flows the white water.
Here we part, friend, once forever.
You go ten thousand miles, drifting away
Like an unrooted water-grass.
Oh, the floating clouds and the thoughts of a wanderer!
Oh, the sunset and the longing of an old friend!
We ride away from each other, waving our hands,
While our horses neigh softly, softly. . . .

—OBATA SHIGEYOSHI (1922)

Obata Shigeyoshi 小畑 薫良 (1888–1971) graduated from the
University of Wisconsin in 1914, where he also earned a mas-
ter's degree in English a few years later. During that time, he
published a few poems in student magazines, which oozed
with sentimentality. ("Oh, what fills my eyes with bitter
tears?/Oh, what fills my heart with ghastly fears?" Yeah,
that's a real quote.) They're almost as painful to read as my
college poetry. But when *Cathay* came out the year after he
graduated, with both its "extravagant errors" and "abundant
color, freshness, and poignancy," as Obata put it, he was in-
spired to venture into free-verse translations of his own with
admirable success: "I confess it was Pound's little book that
exasperated me and at the same time awakened me to the
realization of new possibilities."

Obata stands out in this crowd because of his early edu-
cation in Japan: "I am a Japanese. I pretend to no erudition
in Chinese literature. But I have been all my life a student
and lover of Chinese poetry, or as much of it as I can read.
In my boyhood I learned some shorter pieces of Li Po by
heart. And during these past years of my study and travel in
America I have always carried with me a small edition of his
works." Obata may be an amateur compared with Giles and
Zottoli, but that's more than they could do as boys.

Yet what this anecdote does not reveal is that when Obata
recited those "shorter pieces" from memory as a boy—let's
say, the four-line "Seeing Off Meng Haoran for Guangling
at Yellow Crane Tower" 黄鶴樓送孟浩然之廣陵—the young
Shigeyoshi was not reciting the characters in Mandarin or any
other Chinese dialect but using the Japanese *on'yomi* 音読み
(sound-readings) of the kanji. These alternate Sino-Japanese
pronunciations entered the Japanese language during the
Tang dynasty, when classical Chinese was an erudite lingua
franca in Asia, not unlike Latin in medieval and renaissance
Europe, so they sometimes preserve Tang-dynasty rhymes

that were later lost in the evolution of Chinese. (How cool is that?) Thus, instead of reciting the first line of the poem just mentioned 故人西辭黃鶴樓 as *guren xici Huanghelou*, Obata would have said *kojin seiji Kokaku ro*. That's how Pound found the line transcribed in the notes Fenollosa took during his lessons in Japan and why Pound's version of that poem begins: "Ko-jin goes west from Ko-Kaku-ro." The point is not that Obata is wrong but that his contact with Li Bai, like Pound's, was mediated through Japanese.

I'd also hazard a guess that the "small edition" Obata mentions was not a Chinese edition he happened to find in a bookshop in Wisconsin in 1910 but rather a Japanese anthology from home, which would have been extensively annotated with marginal glosses in Japanese using the traditional *kundoku* 訓読 (gloss-reading) method, more or less allowing Obata to read the poems as though they were Japanese.

I think it's no coincidence that of all the translators we have seen so far, only Giles, Pound, and Obata have given us *blue* mountains instead of "green" ones. Remember, *qing* 青 signifies a spectrum, the "color of nature." It's what linguists now call a "grue," or GREEN+BLUE. (Think of how the two colors blend into each other on a color wheel, between BLUE and YELLOW.) In Chinese, *qing* 青 typically (but not always) means GREEN, while in Japanese (pronounced as *sei* セイ or *ao* あお), it typically (but not always) means BLUE. In other words, the Japanese meaning of the character 青 may have nudged Obata and Pound (via Mori) toward BLUE.

Obata's *lie beyond* is the most lucid and eloquent description yet for what the *mountains* do (橫) to the *north wall*. But he reverses the syntax of the second line into a chiasmus or crossing pattern:

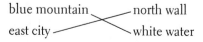

The inverted syntax has an olde-fashion'd poesie feel: *Round the city's eastern side flows the white water.* Why not, "White water flows around the city's eastern side"? Straight-forward, idiomatic, parallel. Line 3 calls to the *friend* directly, and the stakes are raised by adding *forever* to *once* (一). The *unrooted water-grass* is explicitly connected to the friend in a smooth simile with no hint of dude ranchers or Wisconsin dairy farmers. Not bad. Obata ingeniously solves the problem of the paratactic neck (3rd) couplet with a Victorian ejaculation (i.e., "A short hasty emotional utterance," *OED* 4b): *Oh!* This allows him to present all the terms in the couplet without having to decide how they are related while also recreating the parallelism: *Oh, the floating clouds AND the thoughts!/Oh, the sunset AND the longing!* Verbs are not required in Victorian ejaculations.

Both wave. In Obata's vivid embellishment, they also both *ride away from each other*. Not one, but both *horses neigh*, and not *laut* as in Forke, but *softly, softly*, like the windy, swishy, onomatopoeic repetition of *xiao-xiao* 蕭蕭, trailing off with a quiet ellipsis . . .

12

"Je reconduis un ami," Bruno Belpaire

La montagne verte fait face au faubourg du Nord
  et les eaux claires entourent la ville, à l'Est.
A cette place une fois (nous nous) séparâmes et
  (sa) voile solitaire (pour) dix mille li (est) partie.
Les nuages qui errent (provoquent mes) pensées
  (sur) celui (qui est) à l'étranger et le soleil qui
  descend (évoque) le souvenir de (mon) ami intime.
Il a agité la main, il est parti d'ici . . . (ma) tristesse
  profonde (est dans) le hennissement de mon cheval.

Note: Le cheval d'auteur hennit et dans cet appel
  de la bête, il retrouve comme un écho de
  l'appel intérieur de son coeur à lui.

—BRUNO BELPAIRE (1921)

I Escort a Friend

The green mountain faces toward the neigh-
    borhood in the North and the clear waters
    surround the city, to the East.
At this place one time (we) separated and (his)
    solitary sail (for) ten thousand li (has) departed.
The wandering clouds (provoke my) thoughts
    (about) him (who is) far away and the setting
    sun (evokes) the memory of (my) dear friend.
He waved his hand, he departed from
    here . . . (my) deep sadness (is in) the whinny-
    ing of my horse.

Note: The author's horse whinnies, and in this
    animal call he finds an echo of the inner call
    of his own heart.

Bruno Belpaire (1885–1979) was a Belgian sinologist and cofounder of L'Institut belge des hautes études chinoises (Belgian Institute of Higher Chinese Studies) in 1929. His voluminous translations of prose and poetry were harshly criticized by the world's top sinologists, but that's what happens when you bat in the big leagues.

Belpaire uses the sinological method of placing in parentheses everything that has been inferred by the translator as opposed to translated directly. My version in Chapter 4 is a madhouse take on the same method. But while mine is unreadable because it presents all possible alternatives simultaneously, Belpaire's is more selective, more legible, and more compromised. If, for example, we discard the interpolated subject in parentheses from *(nous nous) séparâmes* ([we] separate [from each other]), it boomerangs back in the first-person plural conjugation of *séparâmes*, as though it were inevitable. (By contrast, *separate* in English could be governed by *you*, *we*, or *they*.) Admittedly, this limitation is part of the method, so informed readers learn to read around it. Strangely, however, Belpaire drops the sinological parentheses at the end of the poem, where they are most needed: *Il a agité la main, il est parti d'ici* (He waved his hand, he left from here). The lack of parentheses misleadingly suggests that the Chinese explicitly states that it is the friend who *waved* 揮 and *departed* 去. We'd be fooled if we couldn't consult the Chinese.

The verb tenses work the same way. Ideally, in a method like this, every time the translator makes a limiting decision of any kind it would be flagged with brackets, but there's no elegant way to do that with verb tenses. Belpaire thus shifts back and forth between present and past tenses without flagging his inferences: lines 1–2 depict the poet in the present, lines 3–4 recall the poet's past, lines 5–6 depict the poet in the present recalling the past, and lines 7–8 recall the past again. Thus, instead of a scene of farewell unfolding in the

moment, the whole poem is recast into a sort of Proustian
search for lost times, a remembrance of friends past. Li Bai's
tea and madeleine are the floating clouds and the setting sun
that *provoquent* his *pensées* (意, thoughts) and *évoque* his *sou-
venir* (for 情, emotion). Both of these lines are centered on the
subjectivity of the poet (as in Gautier) instead of split between
the thoughts of the traveler and the emotions of the poet (as
in Giles, Forke, and Obata). Another possibility would be for
these two images to portray the conflicted identity of the poet's
traveling friend: As a traveler he "thinks" like the clouds about
to float away, but as a friend he "feels" like the sun setting with
finality. That is also a viable reading, part of the poem's layers
of polysemy. Nobody, however, to my knowledge, has ever
translated it that way.

Then, *(ma) tristesse profonde (est dans) le hennissement de
mon cheval* ([my] deep sadness [is in] the neighing of my horse).
Belpaire's conjecture that the line is about the poet's deep sad-
ness (*ma*, my)—and not, say, the horse's deep sadness—is put
in its proper (parenthetical) place, but the Chinese nowhere
specifies *mon* (my) for *cheval* (horse). That's another inference
generated from the Proustian scene of remembrance in which
the poet has returned alone to the sad spot of separation on
horseback. My point is not that he's wrong but that he fails to
flag that limiting decision with the brackets he uses elsewhere.
The final line is certainly melancholy, but unless Belpaire
knows more Equinese than I do, translating *xiao-xiao* as *(ma)
tristesse profonde* is as *jambon*-handed as you can get, smash-
ing the ending's delicate implication of an inexpressible grief
at parting, which is precisely what has always been so admired
about this poem. Li Bai's *tristesse* here is as deep and clear as
a white river, yet Belpaire still seems to think it cries out for a
footnote to echo the call. That's the kind of sadness you feel
deep in your horse.

13

"Le chanson d'adieu," Jean-Marie Guislain

Sur le vert décor de la montagne
se découpe le donjon du nord;
l'eau claire entoure le mur de l'est.
Au gré d'une voile solitaire,
pour voyager d'innombrables lieues,
c'est d'ici qu'hélas! il est parti!

Errant où son caprice le pousse,
flottant nuage, au coucher du jour,
l'ami le plus cher m'abandonna;
nos mains s'étant disjointes enfin,
le bruit même des eaux remuées
soupirait une chanson d'adieu.

—JEAN-MARIE GUISLAIN (1925)

The Song of Farewell

Against the green backdrop of the mountain
the north tower cuts a figure;
the clear water surrounds the east wall.
With the help of a solitary sail,
to travel to innumerable places,
it is from here, alas! that he departed!

Wandering wherever his whim pushes him,
floating cloud, at the setting of the sun,
my dearest friend abandoned me;
our hands having been finally pulled apart,
even the noise of the troubled waters
sighed a song of farewell.

Belpaire and Jean-Marie Guislain (1882–1969) were both Francophone Belgians (what *is* it with Li Bai and the Belgians?), but they were about as different as, well, two Belgian translators of Li Bai can be. Belpaire was a career sinologist. Guislain was an itinerant portrait painter and the author of several books of poetry who heroically rescued a wealthy widow in Nebraska from her wrecked home after a tornado, married her daughter, adopted the pseudonym Joseph Leonard, hung out in Paris, and retired in L.A. He couldn't read Chinese.

But he knew someone who did, C. F. Yau 姚昌復 (1884–1963), a connoisseur of rare Chinese art and antiques and later president of the importers Tong-Yin & Co., Paris, New York. Guislain thus belongs to the modernist vogue for translingual collaboration, the uniqueness of which should not be underestimated. Historically, translators have been expected to be able to read the language they are translating. (Well, duh.) But Pound changed all that. It's true that entrepreneurial poets had sometimes derived new translations from old ones without reading the originals, but Pound set a new precedent by translating from authoritative, word-for-word cribs — something putatively closer to the text, or at least to the active mind of an informed reader, than a finished translation might be. The subtitle of *Cathay* boasts this: "from the notes of the late Ernest Fenollosa, and the decipherings of the Professors Mori and Ariga." Not derivation but a distant collaboration with experts. Guislain makes a similar boast: *Une transcription de Li-Taï-Peh. D'après les caractères traduits et commentés par Yau Chang-Foo* (A transcription of Li Taibai. Based on characters translated and annotated by Yao Changfu). Not just a translation, mind you, but a *transcription*. From *characters*. Which have been *translated* and also *commented upon*. By a real *Chinese* guy. Jo Leo out-Cathays *Cathay*.

If Guislain's notes from Yau were anything like Pound's, he seems similarly to have felt free to crib his cribs as the Muse commanded, "transcriptions" be *damnées*. Indeed, the freest translations are always by those who least know the language, for better or for worse. To his credit, Guislain invents a coherent imagistic scheme for his new poem: The river *water* from the head couplet flows into the *solitary sail* (as in Giles, Gautier, Fletcher, and Belpaire), then eddies back at the end as *troubled waters* that come alive and *sighed a song of adieu* (hélas). In the original, the horses don't need to be anthropomorphized to suggest inexpressible human emotion, though I hasten to add that it wouldn't be a fault if they were. The ideal is the indirectness of it. But is this hippophobia really necessary? "Xiao xiao," I say. (I say again, "Xiao xiao.")

Guislain's version, like Belpaire's, is a scene of remembrance. His Li Bai is also a bit of a drama queen, *abandoned* by his dearest friend as their *hands* are *pulled apart*. The *cloud* is a metaphor for the friend, but the *sunset* is real. No "thoughts" or "emotions" necessary.

Three translators so far have given us some form of "clear water" for *baishui* 白水: Zottoli (*limpida*), and Belpaire and Guislain (*claire*). They're not wrong, since *bai* 白 can mean "white," "bright," or "clear." (In fact, the term is still used for clean drinking water.) But are they right? And why only these three translators? It may be no coincidence that when you order a *vino bianco* in Naples or a *vin blanc* in Brussels, you can see right through the carafe. It's not "white" like milk but clear, cool, and refreshing. (These continental fellas may be on to something.) If you've ever attended a Chinese banquet, you've seen *baijiu* 白酒. That means "white wine," but it looks like vodka and packs almost the same punch. Clearly, more research is needed.

14

"Farewell to a Friend," Henry Hart

Where misty blue mountains loom dim in the north,
And the eastern wall rears its high gate,
Where down the green stream drops a lone fisher craft,
There I watched you ride off to your fate.

The clouds drifted lazily far overhead,
Snow-white sails on an ocean of blue.
Your horse bore you from me for ever and aye,
As I waved a last farewell to you.

Hot tears my eyes blinded,
And dim drew the sun;
From the mountains the north wind blew chill.
The glad day was ended, swift came on black night,
As you vanished from sight o'er the hill.

—HENRY HART (1931)

Henry Hart (1886–1974), Bay Area lawyer turned anthropological adventurer, traveled widely in Asia, wrote books on Marco Polo and the Portuguese voyages to India, lectured briefly at UC-Berkeley on Chinese history and art, and published three collections of Chinese poetry in translation. He knew classical Chinese, but it's hard to say how well. He clearly had a strong creative streak, since he reorganizes and prints the Chinese text for a few other classical poems as if they had been written in free verse. They're so wacky, you gotta love 'em. He says he consulted Giles, Forke, and Armand Gandon (we'll come to him) and presumably others: Gautier's clouds, you'll recall, also drift *lazily*, though there is no such word in the Chinese.

Hart's translation bounces along in anapestic tetrameters (da-da-*dump*, da-da-*dump*, da-da-*dump*, da-da-*dump*) with alternating rhymed trimeters, which these days unfortunately sound more like Doctor Seuss than Lord Byron. Time has not been kind to the anapest. Not a slave to form, Hart steals a trick out of the free-verse handbook and breaks the first line of the last stanza to let his half line breathe, but then resumes the meter again. As in Giles, he uses the past tense for emotions recollected in tranquility from the poet's writing desk, whereas Belpaire and Guislain send the poet back out into the field to trigger the post-traumatic nostalgia.

Hart's color palette is the same as the original but all mixed up, as if the spaniel knocked over the easel and the butler botched the tidy up. Following Giles, Hart gives us *blue* mountains for *qing* 青 ("grue"), but then recovers the lost viridity of that move in the next line with a *green* stream for *bai* 白 (white), after which he recovers the lost nividity of *that* move with *snow-white sails*, as if the *gu peng* 孤篷 (lone sail) had split off into the *lone fisher craft* in line 3, then continued to multiply. But take note, these are not real *sails* but rather (metaphor alert) billowing *clouds* in the sky's

ocean of blue. We know the *fisher craft* is part of the land-
scape, not the means of escape, because we're immediately
told that the poet *watched* the friend *ride off*—you know,
hippokinetically.

The horse is put before the wave. The friend gets the
horse, the poet gets the wave. No whinnying, neighing, or
nickering of any kind. In fact, Hart wraps it all up in two
stanzas, then adds an extra stanza just for the poet's grief.
The *hot tears* forge a new opposition with the *chill* of the
north wind coming off those *mountains* in the *north* first
mentioned in line 1, which in turn seem related to the *hill*
over which the friend *vanished*. Like Guislain, Hart seems
to feel the need to gather up all the loose ends, but the aes-
thetic ideal of Tang poetry is for open-endedness and linger-
ing echoes.

Hart's *green stream*, I confess, really bugs me because it
dodges the conundrum of *baishui* 白水 (white/clear + wa-
ter/river). Mori's cribs, by the way, show he thought *white*
meant "bright" because of the reflection of the sunset on the
river's surface. That's a solid reading. Pound ignored him.
You'd think a frothy "white" might make the best parallel
for another color word, but the obliqueness of the parallel-
ism is part of its beauty, as if to say this *green* (which means
blue) is set against this *white* (which means *clear* or *bright*).
Scholars call this "borrowed parallelism" 借對. The poetic
electricity arcs across the gap between signifier and signified,
where surfaces are belied by depths of meaning. But there's
another twist.

Baishui 白水 is the old name for the river flowing along
the eastern side of the famous walled city of Nanyang—also
called *Baihe* 白河, using the more common word for "river"
河, but with the same meaning. (See the map.) Yu Moun-
tain 豫山, directly north of the old city, was and is also called
Lone Mountain 獨山. Li Bai knew them both well. In a

Figure 1. Detail of a two-page schematic map of the city of Nanyang and its
environs, from the *Nanyang County Gazetteer* 南陽縣志 (1693). This map
may be a thousand years after Li Bai walked the streets of Nanyang, but
as Du Fu would not be surprised to learn: 山河在, the mountains and the
rivers are still there. (Can you believe it?) Image courtesy of the Harvard-
Yenching Library, Harvard University, digital repository.

poem called "Visiting Nanyang's 'White' River, I Climb the
Rocks and Am Moved to Write This," he writes: "Wading
at dawn into the source of the 'White' River / I find a brief
respite from the human throng." Another begins: "It was
evening in the city of Nanyang. / I ate a solitary meal of
ferns on Lone Mountain / and recalled a time with Cui
Zongzhi, / punting in the 'White' [Clear] River with a pale
moon" 昔在南陽城，唯餐獨山蕨，憶與崔宗之，白水弄素月.

In short, the parallelism of *green* and *mountain* draws the sense of *white* and *water* out of "Clear River"—the proper name dissolving into a color and an object, then coalescing again into a proper name, back and forth, over and over. Surface and depth. An unnamed place, then a place with a private history and a name. Li Bai's older contemporary Wang Zhihuan 王之渙 (688–742) does something similar when he writes: "The 'white' sun disappears, leaning on the mountain./The 'yellow' river flows, entering the ocean" 白日依山盡, 黄河入海流. A "white" sun is a bright sun, but the "yellow" river is not just *any* yellow river: it's *the* Yellow River.

And now that I mention it, here's one of the two poems I just cited about Nanyang's *Baishui* 白水, in its entirety:

Visiting Nanyang's "White" River, I Climb the Rocks and Am Moved to Write This

Wading at dawn into the source of the "White" River,
I find a brief respite from the human throng.

Islands and islets
        have the look of lovely realms.
The river's sky
        envelopes pure emptiness.

My gaze rises
        reaching the clouds over the sea.
My mind relaxes
        playing with fish in the stream.

I sing loudly until the last of the sun sets,
then take the moon home to my country shack.

遊南陽白水登石激作

朝涉白水源，　暫與人俗疏。島嶼佳境色，　江天涵清虛。
目送去海雲，　心閒遊川魚。長歌盡落日，　乘月歸田廬。

This is what is called an "old style" poem 古體詩, which means it doesn't follow the strict metrical rules of the "new-style" (or "recent-style") poetry 近體詩 demanded by the sonnet. (We'll talk meter in Chapter 23, so hold your soughing horses for now, my nerdlings.) Otherwise, it follows the sonnet form perfectly: (A) one couplet of chatty verse introducing a scene with the poet in it, (B) two couplets of parallel verse describing the external world and indirectly evoking the poet's condition, then (C) one final couplet in chatty verse bringing us directly back to the poet. Note how full lines and broken lines are used in my translation to distinguish between the two kinds of couplet. Technically, the chin (second) couplet has only a "flowing" parallelism (*lovely* 佳 and *envelopes* 涵 are not grammatical pairs), but it has the *feel* of parallelism. This poem may be in "old style" meter, but it moves like a typical Chinese sonnet.

15

"A Farewell to a Friend," Witter Bynner and Kiang Kang-hu

With a blue line of mountains north of the wall,
And east of the city a white curve of water,
Here you must leave me and drift away
Like a loosened water-plant hundreds of miles. . . .
I shall think of you in a floating cloud;
So in the sunset think of me.
. . . We wave our hands to say good-bye,
And my horse is neighing again and again.
—WITTER BYNNER AND KIANG KANG-HU (1929)

The Jade Mountain is probably the most popular book of Tang poetry in English ever printed, and bits and pieces of it can be found all over the internet. Ezraphiles might grumble that it pales in comparison with *Cathay*, but sinologists like Arthur Waley and Burton Watson praised it for striking a good balance between accuracy and readability (two highly subjective terms), which is due to the divided labors of its two authors, listed in the formulaic subtitle: *Translated by Witter Bynner* [1881–1968] *from the Texts of Kiang Kang-hu* [江亢虎, 1883–1954].

Bynner was a well-heeled Harvard man and quasi-bohemian poet who socialized with the artistic and literary illuminati of the day. He traveled with D. H. Lawrence, poured a mug of beer over Robert Frost's head (for teasing him about being gay), and was briefly engaged to Edna St. Vincent Millay. He marched in the streets for women's rights and supported Langston Hughes and Countee Cullen with a prize for younger poets. In 1918, he was teaching English to recruits in Berkeley as a conscientious objector to the war.

Kiang was an energetic political thinker and activist who knew multiple languages; traveled in Japan, Europe, North America, and Russia; and held various government posts. He was an early advisor to Yuan Shikai, founded the Chinese Socialist Party, met with Lenin, championed women's rights, founded a university in Shanghai, founded a Chinese studies program in Montréal, consulted for the Library of Congress in Washington, blasted Pearl Buck in the *New York Times*, and finally joined the collaborationist government against Chiang Kai-shek in 1940 at the request of Wang Jingwei himself. After the Japanese surrender in 1945, he was thrown in prison as a traitor, where he died from malnutrition nine years later. In 1918, however, he, too, was lecturing at UC-Berkeley.

Even as a boy, Kiang stunned scholars with his ability to recite enormous portions of the canonical anthology known as *Three Hundred Tang Poems* 唐詩三百首, culled in the eighteenth century from a total of some 49,000 poems. (Not a typo.) Bynner knew no Chinese but was tuned in to the vogue for Chinese poetry, and he was impressed by Kiang's mastery of Tang verse: "*Cathay*, printed in London three years before, contained passages arrestingly fine," but Kiang "recited offhand versions of the same poems Pound had chosen, which I found, even in Kiang's halting English, still finer." Bynner proposed translating some Wang Wei together. Kiang had a better idea: all 311 poems in the canonical anthology. It took them eleven years.

With a blue line of mountains north of the wall,/And east of the city a white curve of water. The two verbs in the first couplet—*heng* 横 (go across) and *rao* 繞 (go around)—apparently feel too simple and unpoetic for some translators, which would explain why we end up with dynamic verbs like *rearing, looming, cutting, opposing, girding, swelling, surrounding, flowing,* and *enclosing*. But the beauty of the original lies in how the parallelism contains difference within sameness: The first is straight and still, the second curving and dynamic. Bynner elegantly captures this by turning the verbs into nouns within subordinate clauses: *a blue line of mountains, a white curve of water.*

I shall think of you in a floating cloud;/So in the sunset think of me. Bynner's approach to this tricky couplet is equally clever. Remember, the original reads: "Floating cloud, traveler's thoughts./Setting sun, friend's emotions." Parataxis. Nothing to connect the parts. Bynner replaces "traveler" 遊子 with *you* and "friend" 故人 with *me*, making the terms explicit and personal. Like Zottoli, he squeezes a verb (*think of*) out of "thoughts" 意 but repeats it for "emotions" 情. Uniquely, his *floating cloud* and *sunset* become potential future reminders of the present with that declaration (*I shall think of you*), followed by an imperative (*think of me*). There's no question that

Bynner radically alters the meaning of the original, yet he also evokes the implicit association of the landscape with the two friends, along with their intimacy.

For both of these couplets, however, Bynner ditches the parallelism for chiasmus, just as Obata had done. The perfectly parallel *line* and *curve* we just saw is criss-crossed with the rest of the couplet. Why not write, "With a blue line of mountains north of the wall,/And a white curve of water east of the city"? Straight-forward, idiomatic, parallel. Why not write, "I shall think of you in a floating cloud;/So think of me in the setting sun"? What's wrong with that?

Fair is foul and foul is fair. Suit the action to the word, the word to the action. All you need is love. Chiasmus is a powerful figure, resounding with lyricism even in its simplest form, antimetabole. Shakespeare liked chiasmus. English likes chiasmus. Nothing says poetry in English like chiasmus. Yet except for a brief period in the 1580s and the rise and fall of Alexander Pope, parallelism has been a hard sell in English, which has deterred poets from showing the deep structure of Tang verse in translation.

16

"J'ai reconduit mon ami . . . ," Tchou Kia Kien and Armand Gandon

Voici la verte montagne qui barre les faubourgs
    du Nord, et les eaux limpides entourant la
    partie orientale de la ville.
C'est là qu'un jour nous nous sommes quittés.
    Sa voile solitaire partait pour dix mille "li".
Un nuage flottant [passe], symbole du lointain
    voyageur, et le soleil qui se couche évoque en
    moi le souvenir de l'ami.
Il est parti d'ici en agitant la main, et nos che-
    vaux hennissaient tristement.
            —TCHOU KIA KIEN AND ARMAND GANDON (1927)

I Escorted My Friend . . .

Here is the green mountain barring off the
　　neighborhoods in the North, and the limpid
　　waters surrounding the eastern part of the city.
It is here that one day we left each other. His
　　solitary sail departed for ten thousand "li."
A floating cloud [passes], symbol of the distant
　　traveler, and the setting sun evokes in me the
　　memory of the friend.
He departed from here waving his hand, and our
　　horses whinnied sadly.

Sacré bleu, the French love their Chinese poetry, don't they? (It ain't called *chinoiserie* for nothin'.) By 1927, when this poem appeared in a little anthology, Tchou Kia-kien 朱家煙 was known in French as the coauthor of a study on Chinese theater and the translator of an ancient work of Chinese philosophy, as well as the author of a popular manual on mahjong. Armand Gandon (1901–1998) was a French diplomat in his twenties stationed in Kunming.

Gandon's disappointing preface repeats the old French duck that translations of poetry are either *too scholarly*, so they feel like sitting through a bad lecture, or *too literary*, pandering to readers with "fanciful embroideries on translations" and also "almost always *inexactes*." This book, we are promised, finally avoids these two extremes and shows us *"l'esprit chinois* in its true light." And it comes with a guarantee: "We can guarantee the *rigoureuse exactitude* of the translations." *Le diplomate* doth protest too much, methinks. The book also includes a superb introduction and the Chinese text, undoubtedly both prepared separately by Tchou.

And yet for all the talk, Gandon's translation walks like Belpaire's and quacks like Belpaire's. He reduces the eight-line poem to four by fusing the couplets into single lines, like Belpaire. He translates *qing* 情 (emotion) as *souvenir*, like Belpaire. And even though the Chinese text supplied by Tchou uses *peng* 蓬 (tumbleweed)—right there on the page!—Gandon gives us *voile* (sail), like Belpaire. His waters are *limpides*, like Belpaire's rare *claire*. Even his title, *J'ai reconduit mon ami*, is but the past tense of Belpaire's *Je reconduis un ami* with a sly tweak to *my* friend. And there's more synonymizing within the same frame: *montagne verte* to *verte montagne*, *neighborhood* to *neighborhoods* (not "rampart"), *one time* to *one day* (not "once"), *li* to li, etc. Too much is the same. It reads like an artful work of undergraduate plagiarism, paraphrased just enough to foil the phrase-matching app: *and the setting sun (evokes) the memory of (my) dear friend* to *the setting sun evokes in me the memory of the friend*. We've seen enough translations by now to know that even simple lines rarely come out anything alike, and this line is not simple. To be sure, nobody will lament that *Our horses whinny sadly* replaces *(my) deep sadness (is in) the whinnying of my horse*. But where else could that *tristesse* have come from if not Belpaire? *L'esprit chinois*?

If you're willing to put all your cards on the table, then reinventing somebody else's reinvention—even if you can't read the original at all—is a perfectly legitimate mode of poetic production. *After so-and-so*, you say, or *based upon the version by*, or *adapted from the prose of*. Caveat lector; be fruitful and versify. But when both authors are combined into a single byline without naming the actual source, they seem to merge into a unified authority. The resulting Frankanslator is not just some ambitious poet plagiarizing stuff, we think, but the best of both worlds: not adaptation but "real" collaborative translation with a poetic flair. Gandon's versions unquestionably sound better than Belpaire's, partly because Belpaire wasn't interested in sounding good. But the disingenuousness of Gandon's preface, with its dissonance between the soaring rhetoric and the actual poetic practice, rings hollow. And yet it does highlight the patience and resolution with which Bynner reportedly badgered Kiang to check and recheck his revisions. Kiang was a busy man, and for most of their collaboration by correspondence in an age of steamer mail, he was thousands of miles away in Shanghai. Their poems were at least an actual collaboration, though often a "distant" one.

Gandon does another witless thing. Remember that Belpaire (well, unforgettably) had written: *The wandering clouds (provoke my) thoughts (about) him (who is) far away*. Gandon gives: *A floating cloud [passes], symbol of the distant traveler*. After clearing out all those scholarly scare brackets, Gandon puts one—just one—back in, as if he were a painstaking sinologist anxious to flag the one tiny liberty he took with the text: the *cloud [passes]*. But why bracket this and not the addition of *symbole du* (symbol of) or *évoque en moi* (evokes in me) right afterward? *Quel* poser.

Tchou's introduction nicely explains what parallelism is but then dismisses the possibility that it could be anything but repetitive, clumsy, or linguistically logy in translation (*des répétitions ou des lourdeurs*). But poetry is repetition at its core. Can't we at least *learn* to appreciate this quality of Chinese poetry in English translation? How will we know, if we don't try?

17

"Saying Farewell to a Friend," Robert Payne

The green mountain lies beyond the north wall
   of the city,
Where the white water winds in the east—
Here we part.
The solitary sail will attempt a flight of a thousand *li*,
The flowing clouds are the dreams of a wandering son,
The setting sun, the affection of an old friend.
So you go, waving your hands—
Only the bark of a deer.

—ROBERT PAYNE (1947)

I've never been bitten by a deer, but I'm certain its bark is much worse.

Described by one *New York Times* critic as "a literary phenomenon of astounding industry and versatility," the English-born Robert Payne (1911–1983) translated from nine languages (Russian foremost) and churned out over a hundred books, including biographies of Adolf Hitler and Mao Zedong after personally interviewing both. He chaired the translation committee for PEN International and cofounded the Translation Center at Columbia University. His output was always incredible, but 1947 was an especially good year, in which he published an anthology of Chinese poetry and seven other books. At the time, he was married to Rose Hsiung, whose father had served briefly as premier of China.

Payne was a voracious learner, but his command of classical Chinese was never good enough to translate poetry. Instead, according to Payne's own account, he subcontracted various (scandalously unnamed) Chinese translators to write literal versions of selected poems, which Payne then rewrote in free verse. He claims, like Bynner, to have rechecked his final versions with his translators for accuracy, but the last line of this poem belies that vaunt—unless he annoyed this particular (unnamed) translator enough to get pranked.

Payne confuses the geography while condensing the terms of the opening. The *white water* is located *beyond the north wall* along with the (intriguingly singular) *green mountain*, but it also *winds in the east*. In the Far East? *Here we part* is connected to the opening two lines, which is fine, but Payne's ignorance of the poem's couplet structure makes him cut the second couplet in half, apparently in order to create a series of three images: *lone sail, flowing clouds, setting sun*. (The opposite of Forke's mistake but the same as Lowell and Ayscough's.) European rhetoric favors triads—three terms, often building toward a climax—whereas Chinese favors dyads, two terms, often complementing each other, from the shallowest colloquial phrases to the deepest philosophical concepts. Payne's ignorance and linguistic bias seem to distort his perception of the lines.

Like Gautier, Lowell, and Belpaire, Payne lends an air of exoticism and authenticity by transcribing *li* 里 instead of translating it. A *li* is about 1/3 the length of an English mile, but the *wan* 萬 (ten thousand; countless) makes it clear Li Bai is talking hyperbole, not precise distances. After the directness of *li* it seems odd to reduce 10k to *a thousand*, but Payne may be following his ear. In the calquing of "traveler" 遊子 as *wandering son*, we can see the traces of Payne's word-for-word crib. Sometimes translators calque to reveal the poetic contours of the original; sometimes they calque because they're working too fast or in ignorance. Payne's *dreams* is a splendid solution for *yi* 意 (thoughts), but why are the *clouds* here *flowing*, not floating? Is that more aeromantically auspicious?

So you go, waving your hands. One hand is a wave—ask the queen—but two hands is a tizzy, a burst of excitement in a crowd, a warning you're backing into a mailbox. The single dash is elusive because it's not clear what sort of connection it indicates. Is it equivalence? *You go, waving your hands*—which is really—*only the bark of a deer.* Or is it disjunction? *You go, waving your hands*—then, bam! out of nowhere—*only the bark of a deer.* Payne must have thought he was onto some kind of Zen *kōan.* (What is the sound of one deer barking?)

But the final line of the original is closely modeled on a line from a poem in the ancient *Classic of Poetry* 詩經 called "Chariot Charge" 車攻. In fact, it's exactly the same line except for a single character added smack in the middle, which turns "*xiao-xiao,* the horses cry" 蕭蕭馬鳴 into "*xiao-xiao,* the [separated] horses cry" 蕭蕭[班]馬鳴. The insertion of *ban* 班

(separated) not only changes the meter from ancient tetrasyl-labics into "modern" pentasyllabics suitable for an eighth-century sonnet (Li, you clever devil, you), but it also turns *ma* 馬 (horse) into the compound *banma* 班馬, which is rare enough that it can be traced back to a story from a famous ancient chronical (*Commentary of Zuo* 左傳) in which a military advisor says, "The sound of *ban*-horses means the enemy is retreating" 有班馬之聲, 齊師其遁. The bundled standard commentary by Du Yu 杜預 explains that *ban* 班 means "to divide" (the character shows a knife 刂 dividing two pieces of jade 玉) and also that the horses are crying out because they cannot see each other as they flee in the dark. Whether or not Du Yu was right, this was the commentary Li Bai knew. Thus, with the fusing of two allusions to war horses, the high-spirited whinnying of "Chariot Charge" becomes a melancholy equine plaint. But *ban* 班 also means "speckled," so if you parse it separately from *ma* 馬 you could end up with a "dappled roan." Which is sort of like a spotted deer. Right?

"Bow wow," the deer says, again.

18

語譯 (Paraphrase), Xu Zhengzhong

遠看青翠的山巒，橫亙在城北；近見白浪的水面，環繞著城東。我倆一旦在這兒分別後，你就像無根的蓬草一樣，獨自飄流到萬里以外的地方去了！你那遊子的心情與行跡，飄忽不定，如天上的浮雲；而我對你的戀戀難捨，也就像造落日餘暉一樣，依戀在山谷之間，但也難以挽留。我倆揮著手兒，就此分別。你漸行漸遠，只聽到你的坐騎還在蕭蕭地鳴叫！

—XU ZHENGZHONG 許正中 (2004)

In the distance [I/we] see a verdant mountain range stretching out to the north of the city; nearby [I/we] watch the white waves on the surface of the water surrounding the east of the city. After we two leave each other in a moment, you, like a rootless tumbleweed, will go off alone drifting to places thousands of miles away! Your moods and your path as a traveler will wander endlessly like [a] floating cloud[s] in the sky; and my deep sorrow at parting from you will be like the afterglow of the setting sun which reluctantly lingers amidst the mountain valleys but cannot be persuaded to stay. Both of us waving a hand, we separate here. You move gradually farther and farther away until all I can hear is your mount still crying *xiao xiao*!

Chinese readers also use translations of Tang poetry.

If you're reading this, then it's a good bet you were forced to read some Shakespeare in school, and like everyone else you probably struggled and used all the footnotes, summaries, and online paraphrases you could lay your eyeballs on. Shakespeare's sonnets were published in 1609. Li Bai may have written this sonnet around 735 (that's a guess), nearly a thousand years earlier. Nobody speaks this Chinese anymore, if they ever did. Tang poetry is at least as hard as Shakespeare, and most Chinese editions and websites include full "intralingual" translations like the one above, which render the *guwen* 古文 (classical language) of the poems into modern *baihua* 白話 ("white" speech; that is to say, *clear* speech).

And yet—to digress for a moment—it's nothing less than astonishing that a Chinese reader can pick up this poem, read it aloud in any dialect, and get a pretty good idea of what it says. English poetry from the same era sounds like *"Licsar gebad/atol æglæca; him on eaxle wearð/syndolh sweotol,/seonowe onsprungon,/burston banlocan."* That's Beowulf slicing off Grendel's arm, dontcha know, and if you mouth it just right you might get a sprung sinew or a bursting bone-lock out of it, but c'mon: Premodern English is utterly unintelligible to us. Premodern Chinese is not so impenetrable.

Xu Zhengzhong is what we might call a professional amateur, a former engineer who wrote books on Tang poetry in retirement to indulge a lifelong passion: a sensitive, well-informed reader. His mountains are *verdant* 青翠, not blue, and his water has *white waves* 白浪 on the surface, which rationalizes the color. The friend is addressed as *you* and is the one compared to *a rootless tumbleweed*, but Xu's commentary goes on to say: "'Lone tumbleweed' of course refers to the friend or the friend's boat. . . . The sail-fabric of a sailboat is also called 'tumbleweed'; at the same time 'tumbleweed' is a kind of rootless plant." 「孤蓬」當然指友人或友人之舟

而言。. . . 帆船之布帆亦稱「蓬」，同時「蓬」亦是一種無
根之草. Xu assumes that the two different readings result from
synonymous character variants—i.e., *peng* 蓬 (tumbleweed) is
just another way to write *peng* 蓬 (sail). That *can* happen, but
it doesn't seem to be the case here. Xu also divides the neck
couplet explicitly between friend and poet (like Giles, Forke,
and Bynner and Kiang) but elaborates like a Belgian: *my deep
sorrow at parting from you will be like the afterglow of the set-
ting sun which reluctantly lingers amidst the mountain valleys
but cannot be persuaded to stay.* Whoa, filly. (Judith Gautier,
dommage pour toi!) Scholars call this *explicitation*—i.e., mak-
ing *explicit* in translation what is *implicitly* understood by most
readers of the original. It's a useful technique but tricky. Xu's
comment resembles an earlier note by Wang Qi 王琦 (1696–
1774): "Floating clouds move without leaving a trace, and are
thus compared to the traveler's thoughts; the setting sun holds
onto the mountains, hesitantly going, and is thus compared to
the feelings of a dear friend" 浮雲一往而無定跡，故以比遊
子之意；落日銜山而不遽去，故以比故人之情. Both friend
and poet wave and separate, but only the friend's horse neighs.

Pound once observed: "The translation of a poem hav-
ing any depth ends by being one of two things: Either it is
the expression of the translator, virtually a new poem, or it
is as it were a photograph, as exact as possible, of one side of
the statue." Of course, every translation is an interpretation,
but I like this idea of a poem in all its cultural and linguis-
tic complexity as a 3D object that can only be represented
two-dimensionally with other words, including words of the
same language. (The result, however, is a new 3D object of
its own, and so on.) Pound's alternative would be to reinvent it
as "virtually a new poem" from one's own artistic perspective.
But the boundaries blur. One's perspective might be, like a
cubist's, to try to show multiple perspectives at once. A cubist
painting is obviously not an "exact" representation (whatever

that would be), yet gathering together a bunch of translations as we are doing now might be a sort of cubist collage of 2D photographs with various degrees of focus and exposure showing us multiple sides of the sculpture in turn. A patchwork illusion of 3D. Virtually a new poem.

Digression

Peng 蓬 vs. Peng 篷

OK, so one comment of Xu's in the last chapter has been bugging me: "The sail-fabric of a sailboat is also called *tumbleweed*." We know that in the seventeenth century Cao Xuequan printed *peng* 篷 (sail) for *peng* 蓬 (tumbleweed), which most editors have rejected—so why does *sail* 篷 keep popping up? Indeed, why did it pop up in the first place? Cao did sometimes "correct" or "improve" poems. Is that what happened? Or could *sail* 篷 actually be "right"?

The oldest surviving text of Li Bai's poetry dates to the twelfth century. It reads *tumbleweed* 蓬, not *sail* 篷. So, to keep score, that's Tumblers, 1. Sails, 0. The next oldest surviving text was edited by Xiao Shiyun 蕭士贇 in the thirteenth century, who expanded an annotated edition (otherwise now lost) by Yang Qixian 楊齊賢 (fl. 12th c.). Xiao's text also reads *tumbleweed* 蓬. Tumblers, 2. Sails, 0. And he offers a gloss: "The 'lone *peng*' is a weed. Having no roots, it blows and tumbles in the wind, which makes it a good metaphor for a traveler" 孤蓬草也無根而隨風飄轉者自喻客遊也. (Xie xie, Xiao.) His printing of 蓬 (tumbleweed) was therefore no accident. So that's Tumblers, 3. Sails, 0. Indeed, the same term *lone tumbleweed* 孤蓬 appears twice in the sixth-century *Wen xuan* 文選 (Selections of fine literature), an anthology of exemplary writing that Tang poets treated like a literary bible. It occurs in a line by Bao Zhao 鮑照 (414–466) about a desolate landscape where "the *lone tumbleweed* moves on its own" 孤蓬自振 and also in a poem by Wang Sengda 王僧達 (423–458): "The *lone tumbleweed* rolls on frosted roots" 孤蓬捲霜根. Boats don't do that. The literary precedent is irrefutably *tumbleweed*. Tumblers, 5. Sails, 0. (Go, Tumblers!)

But what if Li Bai was riffing, messing with our expectations? Let's do some e-sleuthing. According to a database containing all the (49k) poems in the *Complete Tang Poetry* 全唐詩 edited in 1705, the combination *lone tumbleweed* 孤蓬 appears in a total of 10 poems, and *lone sail* 孤篷 appears in 1.

Yes, 1. And since that poem is an ode to a fishing reel (魯望以 輪鉤相示緬懷高致), I'm not giving it a point, ha. Now we're Tumblers, 15. Sails, 0. Of the other 10, two are by Li Bai. One, of course, is our sonnet. The other reads: "A single person without any support / is a *lone tumbleweed* that *journeys* far. / A thousand miles without any prop / is likewise but a falling leaf" 一身竟無托，遠與孤蓬征。千里失所依，複將落葉並. Both poems use the same verb "to journey" 征. That's probably more than a coincidence in a literary milieu in which a pre- mium was placed on classical allusions, since the same pairing of *tumbleweed* 蓬 and *journey* 征 appears in a famous lyric from the Han dynasty (206 BCE–220 CE): "Light and elegant, the flying *tumbleweed journeys*. / Sad and melancholy, the *trav- eler* yearns" 翩翩飛蓬征，愴愴遊子懷. That's the same *trav- eler* 遊子 whose *thoughts* 意 are the *floating clouds* 浮雲 in our sonnet. Above and beyond the poetic effects we have already discussed, the informed reader will perceive a play of poetic allusions rippling over the surface of the poem, impossible to translate. Tang-dynasty score: Tumblers, 14. Sails, zippo.

Poetic tastes, however, like all tastes, are fickle, and they soon flipped on this point. In the Song dynasty, *lone tumble- weed* 孤蓬 rolls away in 56 poems, but *lone sail* 孤篷 sails away with a whopping 99. Dang. Tumblers, 70. Sails, 99. The trend continues over the next three dynasties (Liao, Jin, and Yuan) with a tumblebush-to-jonk ratio of 5 to 38 (11%), followed by 87 to 159 (31%) in the Ming, and 43 to 137 (24%) in the Qing. Final score: Tumblers, 205. Sails, 433! No wonder *lone sail* 孤篷 keeps cruising back into our poem: It was favored by po- ets in subsequent dynasties 2 to 1, even though Tang-dynasty poets favored the *lone tumbler* 孤蓬 10 to 1. Snap.

And who can blame them? A *lone sail* is a rockin' good poetic image, and Tang poets knew it. The common word for *sail* is *fan* 帆 (as in *fanchuan* 帆船, sailboat), which I'll call a *lugsail* to distinguish it from the *peng* 篷 (sail) in our sonnet: Tang poets used the combination *gu fan* 孤帆 (lone lugsail) a total of 85 times, compared with that one fishing-reel poem with *gu peng* 孤蓬 (lone sail). Including all other poems up through the Qing, *lone lugsail* 孤帆 appears 887 times, twice as many times as *lone tumbleweed* 孤蓬 with 433. Thus, considering the preference for *lone sail* 孤蓬 over *lone tumbleweed* 孤蓬 in *post*-Tang poetry and the popularity of *lone lugsail* 孤帆 in poetry throughout the imperial period, it may be that the melancholy beauty of a solitary sheeted mast as a synecdoche for the vessel of a lonely traveler nudged Cao Xuequan to revise *peng* 蓬 to *peng* 蓬 in Li Bai's poem as a "better" alternative, at least by post-Tang standards. He may even have been influenced by a line of Wang Wei's, which contains 3 of the same 5 characters:

孤帆萬里外   "A *lone lugsail* [goes] for *10k miles* and more" (Wang)

孤蓬萬里征   "A *lone tumbleweed* for *10k miles* journeys" (Li)

By the way, Li Bai does *lugsails*, too. One of the 85 hits just noted is in his own seeing-off poem to Meng Haoran, mentioned in chapter 11: "The distant shadow of [your] *lone lugsail* vanishes into the blue emptiness./All [I] see is the Long River flowing to the edge of the sky" 孤帆遠影碧空盡, 唯見長江天際流. Now there's a fine image. If you were a translator or editor, would you use it *here* because it appeared *there*?

19

"Farewell to a Friend," Adet Lin

Horizontal lies the azure hills across the North,
And the gleaming river goes 'round the eastern town.
The long sail prepares for a journey of a thousand *li*.
As drifting clouds, light and gay the whim
Of the wandering son, and
Wistful as sunset, the sentiments of the elders.
So farewell, and solitary departure.
See, how the bells jangle on the speckled horse.

—ADET LIN 林如斯 (1970)

Adet Lin 林如斯 (1923–1971) had the blessing and curse to be
born the eldest daughter of Lin Yutang 林語堂 (1895–1975),
one of the great literary figures of the twentieth century. She
declared at age seven that she wanted to be a writer like her
father, moved with her family to the United States at age
thirteen, and published her first book (a family biography) at
age sixteen and her first novel at age twenty. She left Colum-
bia University for China after her sophomore year in 1943
to join the war effort against Japan. Later, she eloped with
the ne'er-do-well son of a rich American on the eve of her
own engagement party, which was arranged by her father,
causing a family scandal, but the match was miserable and
ended in divorce. She spent time in a sanatorium, perhaps
suffering from bipolar disorder. In her forties, she worked
as a translator for the National Palace Museum in Taipei,
where this book was published with an affectionate foreword
by her father. She took her life a few months later.

Poems touch and transform lives. We may interact with
them at a gut level or as an intellectual exercise, to various
degrees aware or unaware of the other lives they have touched
or transformed—but the fact remains that at one level this
poem by Li Bai exists as an almost incomprehensibly vast in-
terlingual, intertextual, and interaffective network connecting
countless thousands of people. It strains the imagination to
visualize such a network—less a constellation of stars than
a little galaxy of solar systems radiating and reflecting light. I
have no delusion that what Li Bai first thought and felt when
writing it has anything more than a tangential connection to
what others have often thought and felt when reading it. But if
that poem has an "essence," it can only be manifested through
reinvention. Some reinvention may be appropriation in the
worst sense, but it can also be a reaching out—opening up
and linking into that network of thousands.

Lin is the first to give us an *azure* landscape, which would be a stroke of eloquence if it weren't a reckless swipe at the thesaurus. Green mountains may look bluish in the distance, but *azure* is sky-blue by definition. Yet here be *azure hills*, sky-like, otherworldly. Lin also stands out from the crowd with an elegantly *gleaming* river—the first since Mori to read *bai* 白 as "bright" instead of frothy white or crystal clear. Less originally, Lin inverts the first sentence to make the typical chiasmus (*lies / hills* >< *river / goes*), which also veils the subject-verb disagreement in what would otherwise be "the azure hills lies horizontal" (the *z/ʒ* sounds were too seductive). Then a *long sail*. Lin sides with the sailors instead of the bushwhackers, but I'm guessing that *long* is a typesetter's gaffe for *lone*, reminding us how easy it is for a tiny change like 蓬/篷 to enter a text.

The truly striking features of Lin's version come at the end. First, Lin cuts the original line 3 ("From this place, once we separate"), which makes room for a three-line rendering of the neck couplet, where she calques the compounds so that "traveler" 遊子 becomes *wandering son* (like Payne) and "old friend" 故人 becomes *elders*. Recall from Chapter 3 that *zi* 子 means "son" or "child," but when attached to a verb or adjective it often functions as a nominalizer, transforming it into a noun subject: "to travel" 遊 + 子 = *traveler*. No minors admitted. Likewise, once again, *gu* 故 means "old" (among other things), but when combined with *ren* 人 (person) we get "dear friend." When single words are combined into compounds, the meaning fundamentally changes, but Lin teases out the latent sense of the components like one of Lowell and Ayscough's split-ups, except that she splits up compounds, not characters. Li Bai's poetic grief at his friend's departure is thus completely reinvented as a generational divide between the *light and gay whim* of the young (like *drifting clouds*) and the *wistful sentiments* of the old (like the *sunset*). Are these the howlers of a bilingual speaker untrained in classical Chinese or the intentionally creative reinventions of Tang topoi appropriated into a gloriously bold and tragic life with a keen awareness of youthful follies and mature regrets?

So farewell. No "with a wave, you depart," but this disarmingly simple phrase. Therefore, goodbye. The logic stuns. And *solitary departure*. There's no *solitary* in the original, but the sleek paraphrase avoids the dilemma of who does what. In the end, we all leave alone. *See, how the bells jangle.* Lin's ending is as breathtaking as Gautier's *chant d'oiseau* with just as much method as madness. Since *ming* 鳴 (to cry out) can also be used for the sounding of bells (or the cracking of a whip, for that matter), Lin's horse clears the rails of that annoying double oxer of *xiao-xiao* and *whinny* with a lyrical conjuring of bells sounding discordantly to express grief "beyond the words" 言外. *Speckled* is an intuitive reading of *ban* 班 as a variant of *ban* 斑 (spotted, striped): Lin apparently never saw an edition with footnotes explaining the allusion to *banma* 班馬 (stray horse) and splits up the compound instead. So strange. So lovely. So sad.

20

"Taking Leave of a Friend," Innes Herdan

Blue hills rearing over the north wall;
White water swirling to the east of the city:
This is where you must leave me—
A lone puff of thistledown
        on a thousand mile journey.
Ah the drifting clouds
        and the thoughts of a wanderer!
The setting sun
        and emotions of old friends.
A wave of the hand now
        and you are gone.
Our horses whinnied to each other at parting.

                   —INNES HERDAN (1973)

Educated first at Oxford, then at the School of Oriental and African Studies and at the Universities of Nanjing and Wuhan (1936–1937), the London-born Innes (née Jackson) Herdan (1911–2008) was the first person to translate the whole *Three Hundred Tang Poems* 唐詩三百首 into a European language on her own. She fell in love with China in her twenties and was an ardent and steadfast believer in Maoism—so much so that in her eighties she could still defend the excesses of the Cultural Revolution and blame the United States, Hong Kong, and a rabble of hooligans for the Tian'an men massacre. But her bilingual text is a solid work with many graces, including illustrations by Chiang Yee 蔣彝 (1903–1977), Professor Emeritus of Chinese at Columbia.

Herdan's version is responsive to some of the structural qualities of the verse form. Her head couplet is almost perfectly parallel, but like Giles, she subordinates the verbs into gerunds so the lines run on into the next couplet instead of remaining self-contained. Her *hills* are *blue* (like Pound's, Obata's, and Giles's) and also *rearing*, as if anticipating the horses at the end. Like virtually everyone else (but most notably Obata), she gives the more literal *water* over the idiomatic "river." And she sets it *swirling*, which focuses on the water itself rather than on the lay of the river. Her *thistledown* is a uniquely lyrical substitute for *tumbleweed*, quite lovely, with nary a hint of the Lone Ranger, though perhaps too precious in calling the friend a *lone puff*. Like Pound, Payne, and Lin, her *thousand mile journey* avoids the awkwardly literal "ten-thousand" 萬.

Herdan handles the neck couplet like Obata, with a lusty ejaculation (*lusty* in the old sense, of course: "Of language, eloquence, etc.: Pleasing, agreeable," *OED*, 2e): *Ah, the drifting clouds / and the thoughts of a wanderer!* No need to work out the pronouns in the parataxis. The change in lineation also brilliantly mimics the rhythm of the Chinese line, where a caesura—a "cut" or brief pause—separates the first 2 characters from the remaining 3: "drifting cloud" 浮雲 (2) + "wander-er thoughts" 遊子意 (3); "setting sun" 落日 (2) + "old friend feelings" 故人情 (3). That's a 2 + 3 syllabic pattern. (More on this later.)

The setup for the final line sounds regrettably like a wizard's fell handiwork: *A wave of the hand now/and you are gone.* Poof. (*A lone poof*, we might say.) The final line skirts around any Mother Goose silliness with a plain statement, but the sudden shift to the past tense after the sustained present of the whole scene is puzzling and deflating: *This is where you must leave me. . . . Our horses whinnied to each other.*

Herdan borrows Pound's title, perhaps from Obata, who had borrowed it first. It has a pleasantly formal ring to it, but it suggests that the poet is the one departing, not the friend. That seems wrong to me (and just about everyone else), but Yu Xianhao 郁賢皓 (1933–), who is one of the foremost living experts on Li Bai, disagrees: "The 'drifting cloud traveler' in the poem is a self-reference; therefore it seems the poem's title should be 'Taking Leave of a Friend'" 詩中「浮雲遊子」當為自指，故詩題似應作《別友人》. It's true that poets often refer to themselves as *youzi* 遊子 (traveler, drifter, or wanderer), since Tang aesthetics favor third-person metaphors over first-person pronouns, but it's not a rule. Friends travel, too. Accordingly, Yu also thinks that *tumbleweed* 蓬 in line 4 is self-referential: "The chin couplet indicates the theme: once departed from this place, I myself will float and roll as lonely as a tumbleweed for over ten thousand miles" 頷聯點明題旨，此地一別，自己將孤獨地像蓬草一樣飄轉到萬里之外. But Yu is an outlier. Almost everyone understands the *tumbleweed* (or *sail*) to refer to the (departing) friend, who is therefore also the *drifting cloud*, whereas the *setting sun* refers to the poet (staying behind), who calls himself a "friend." But

Yu may be right. Who's to say for sure whether the generic title may not have been imposed by an early compiler like Yang or Xiao? In the absence of any pronouns, the title largely determines the identities in the metaphors. Change the title, and the poem flips inside-out like a chev'ril glove.

21

"Farewell to a Friend," Xu Yuanchong

Green hills range north of the walled city,
The White River curves along its east.
Once we part here you'll travel far alone
Like the tumbleweed swept by the autumn wind.
A floating cloud—a wayfarer's feeling from home,
The setting sun—the affection of an old friend.
Waving adieu, as you now depart from me,
Our horses neigh, loath to part from each other.

Blue mountains bar the northern sky;
    White river girds the eastern town.
Here is the place to say goodbye;
    You'll drift like lonely thistledown.
With floating cloud you'll float away;
    Like parting day I'll part from you.
You wave your hand and go your way;
    Your steed still neighs, "Adieu, adieu!"

—XU YUANGCHONG (2012)

The venerable Xu Yuanchong 許淵沖 (1921–2021), a long-time professor at Beijing University with some fifty books to his name, was renowned for his many translations of classical poetry into English and French, as well as for his translations of Flaubert, Proust, and Stendhal into Chinese. He survived the Cultural Revolution partly by translating Mao Zedong's sonnets into English. (Yes, even Mao wrote them.) Late in life, he used these two versions to discuss his translation method, describing the first as "more faithful to the word" and the second as "more beautiful and poetical."

That opposition between the "beautiful" and the "faithful" has been the bane of translation for centuries, even when it is not cast as a misogynistic witticism (which I'll not repeat). In part, Xu's point is that rhyme and meter make a translation more "beautiful," but I'd venture to say that his "faithful" version is as beautiful as any of the other free-verse translations we've seen so far—even though it does suffer from a dangling modifier that implies the horses are waving their little hooves to each other (*Waving adieu, . . . Our horses neigh*). So cute.

The genius of the rhyme scheme of the Chinese sonnet is that it strings together the otherwise self-contained couplets on a single rhyme on the even lines, like charms on a friendship bracelet (AB-CB-DB-EB). Instead of trying to recreate that, Xu follows what is typical in traditional English verse (like Giles and Fletcher) by splitting the poem into two quatrains and rhyming on the odd lines as well (ABAB-CDCD). Such a division suits this poem quite well in its relative emphasis on the external and the internal, in turn—first the scene of separation, then the emotions of separating—even though they ultimately blend together.

Xu explains his different choices for the two verbs in the head couplet thus: (In the faithful version) "*range* is a geographic term and *curve* a geometric one, and they are not so beautiful as *bar* or *gird* for the one may be found in Keats' verse *while barred clouds bloom the soft dying day*. And the other may remind us of Edmund Waller's Poem 'On a Girdle.'" Xu's criterion for poetic diction in English is thus the Chinese one of how ingeniously it alludes to other great poetry. Xu also seems to treat related English words like Chinese words, a great many of which can act as noun, verb, or adjective, depending on the context. When Keats uses *barred* as an adjective, he means "with bars" or "streaked," but when Xu uses *bar* as a transitive verb it seems to mean "block off" (*mountains bar the northern sky*). His opaque allusion to Keats doesn't help. And I don't know about you, but I certainly didn't think of Waller's (mildly erotic) seventeenth-century poem on a "girdle" (i.e., a sash) when I read this, and I actually know Waller's poem. The verb *to gird* and the noun *girdle* may be cognates, but they now have *very* different associations. There's also nothing necessarily unpoetic about geographic or geometric terms, at least not anymore. And *range* is a "geographic term" only when used as a noun; as a verb it means "to wander," as in Thomas Wyatt's (mildly erotic) sixteenth-century poem about (alas, the day) beautiful, unfaithful women: "and now they range / Busily seeking with a continual change."

Xu evidently also thinks that *baishui* 白水 refers to *The White River* (as I do), at least when he's thinking faithfully. But when striving for the beautiful, he returns to the generic: "a" *white river* is beautiful; *"the" White River* is not. So, too, *green hills* may be faithful, but they must be *blue* to be beautiful. Those *hills* probably become *mountains* in order to achieve that perfect parallelism, even down to the number of matching syllables: *Blue/White, mountains/river, bar/girds, the/the, northern/eastern, sky/town*. Beautiful. Can we have a round for Prof. Xu? The *sky/town* pairing is in the beautiful version, not the faithful, so nobody's going to grouse over the translation of *guo* 郭 (rampart) as *sky*. (He doesn't even try to make the head couplet parallel in the faithful version, but once again, I think it sounds quite beautiful.)

For that tricky *peng* 蓬, Xu's (faithful) *tumbleweed* becomes Herdan's (beautiful) *thistledown*, though it is just as "faithful," I would argue, as a plant that blows away, and, what's more, that *tumbleweed* in the faithful version is conspicuously beautified (ill phrase, vile phrase, I know, I know) by rendering ten thousand *li* 里 of travel as *swept by the autumn wind*. Whoosh. In fact, Xu admits no journeying or counting of *li* in either version. The parallel neck couplet in the beautiful version sounds a bit too much like pidgin English and Winnie-the-Pooh balloon physics: *With floating cloud you'll float away*. But those dashes in the faithful version make me sit up and pay attention (even if chiasmus does elbow out parallelism once again).

Can we really say which is more beautiful and which more faithful? Faith is always in the eye of the beholder. Most poets must take a leap of beauty. Translators, too.

22

"taking leaves (1)," "parting friend," Harry Gilonis

"quite a way after Li Po"

blue green remembered hills
white water circles walls
here one makes separation
planted uprooted drifting floating
sun down friend old
go from this here
freedom, spontaneity and defiance
noise noise called leaving

parting friend

blue hill horizons north
white water rounds to east
parting taken to be necessary
leaf-litter blown ten thousand miles . . .
cloud floating (thoughts)
sun-dropping (feelings)
(one) waves (one) leaves
hhuun hhuun [neigh-saying] [crying]

—HARRY GILONIS (2010)

The beloved British poet and literary critic Harry Gilonis is known for experimental poetry like this. These two radical reinventions appear in a collection of similar "re-workings," as he calls them, of eight Chinese sonnets (of eight lines each, of course) by eight Tang poets, all of them not just "after" the originals, as we usually say of adaptations, but *quite a way after* them. The game is afoot. Unlike Xu, Gilonis's two poems do not progress from faithful to beautiful but exist in another realm of translingual, transcultural transmutation altogether. Unlike most translations, Gilonis's interlingual poems are richer alongside the originals. We few, we happy few.

Gilonis's canny *blue green remembered hills* draws that elusive "color of nature" into the familiar landscape of the Shropshire Lad: "Into my heart an air that kills / From yon far country blows: / What are those blue remembered hills, / What spires, what farms are those?" Doubters of blue hills, take note: Windsor Forest has got 'em, too, at least according to Mr. Pope, in a parallel couplet worthy of the Chinese sonnet: "Here in full Light the russet Plains extend; / There wrapt in Clouds the blueish Hills ascend." In "parting friend," the singular *blue hill* "verbs" *horizons*, though we only fully realize it when we come to its pair, *rounds*, in the second line—a trick you sometimes see in Chinese parallelism, here recreated in English.

If these two versions progress, it may be toward parallelism. In the first version, Gilonis fuses the last line of the chin couplet with the first line of the neck couplet (as Lowell and Ayscough and also Payne had done), which reduces that pesky varmint of a tumbleweed to its root idea of *planted* and *uprooted*. Similarly, he reduces "floating cloud" 浮雲, "drifter" 遊子, and "thoughts" 意 to *drifting* and *floating*, so that the parallelism with the setting sun in the next line is utterly (how shall I say this?) obnubilated. No feelings in this version either: *sun down friend old*. The inversion of *old friend* to *friend old* feels unflattering to me, and *freedom, spontaneity and defiance* suggests to me that the poet can't wait to get away from the old bugger. YMMV. But the point is that this is a cheeky riff on a crib. That *freedom*, btw, might come from *zi* 自 —part of *ziyou* 自由 (freedom) but here it means "from," as Gilonis surely knows. He also echoes that double *xiao-xiao* with *noise noise*, naming it instead of translating it. The first version appropriates the original with a wink and a nudge, down to the pun in the title, where "taking leaves" acknowledges the stealing of pages.

The second version recreates the parallelism of the neck couplet with bold typography: *cloud floating (thoughts) / sun-dropping (feelings)*. It plays its game of wit but does so along the edges of lyricism. Talking horses? (Wilbur, please.) Here *xiao-xiao* becomes *hhuun hhunn*, what the dappled gray steed says to Gulliver when he arrives in the land of equine enlightenment, that of the rational Houyhnhnms. Like Li Bai's own conflation of classical war horses, the line is best if you get the allusion. For me, the delicious pun in *neigh-saying* (nay-saying, speaking-in-neighs) sounds like an emotionally complex denial of the sad reality of parting, intensified by *crying*. Indeed, *hhuun hhuun* could be a sob or a scoff. In *parting taken to be necessary*, I see *taken to be* as "considered to be," not actually so, suggesting that it is *not* necessary and therefore even more painful for at least one of the two. Only *(one) waves* as the other *(one) leaves*. (YMMV.)

In his preface Gilonis offers a little lesson in literary history, citing John Dryden's (1633–1700) now classic three modes of translation: *metaphrase* (word for word), *paraphrase* (sense for sense), and *imitation* (free adaptation). Of his own poems Gilonis writes: "I cannot call them imitations, as I have often worked closely with the original text; yet without trying to replicate a sensibility, a mood or a theme." FWIW, I'd say the "imitation" category includes not just folks rewriting the translations of others but almost any creative adaptation, including those following calques and cribs down delectably deviant ways, as Gilonis does: re-spect, re-work, re-invent.

Tonal Balance: *Ping* 平 ☺ and *Ze* 仄 ☻

青☺	山☺	橫☺	北☻	郭☻	A	(head)
白☻	水☻	繞☻	東☺	城☺	B	
此☻	地☻	一☻	為☺	別☻	C	(chin)
孤☺	蓬☺	萬☻	里☻	征☺	B	
浮☺	雲☺	遊☺	子☻	意☻	D	(neck)
落☻	日☻	故☻	人☺	情☺	B	
揮☺	手☻	自☻	茲☺	去☻	E	(tail)
蕭☺	蕭☺	班☺	馬☻	鳴☺	B	

Writing a Chinese sonnet is much harder than you'd think.

Every poetic meter is based on the qualities of the language in which it is written. English, for example, has (what we nerds call) an "accentual-syllabic" meter because its accents can be arranged into patterns, like the five syllabic pairs of alternating accents (*iambs*) called "iambic pentameter" (go, nerds!) in which Shakespeare wrote almost everything. Latin, by contrast, has (what we nerds call) a "quantitative" meter because the distinction between long and short vowels is clear in Latin. Chinese, however, has something the others don't. Tones.

The first thing you learn when studying Mandarin is that it has four basic tones, which means that a single syllable — for example, *ma* — can be pronounced four different ways, with four different meanings: *mā* (mother), *má* (hemp), *mǎ* (horse), and *mà* (scold). There's also a neutral tone, which turns *ma* into a question mark, but we don't always count that one. Incidentally, we can see the semiphonetic nature of Chinese script where the character for *mǎ* 馬 (horse) appears as a phonetic indicator in *mā* 媽 (mom), *mà* 罵 (scold), and *ma* 嗎 (question); *má* 麻 (hemp) is the exception. Middle Chinese (MC) also had four tones — confusingly, not the same four tones — but it would be impossibly complicated to have a poetic meter with four options, so those wily medieval poets consolidated them into two classes. The first MC tone, called the *ping* 平 (level) tone, is perceptibly longer than the rest and applies to roughly half of all characters. The remaining three MC tones, which are all shorter, were chucked into a bucket called the *ze* 仄 (oblique) tone. For nerds only: These tones are called "rising tone" 上聲, "falling tone" 去聲, and "entering tone" 入聲, the last of which ends with an unvoiced consonant (*-p, -t,* or *-k*) as in modern Cantonese, which sharply shortens the length of the syllable even more.

The chart here shows the "scansion" or metrical pattern of our poem. Metrical charts typically use ● and ○ for the two MC tone classes, but how boring is that? We're using ☯ to remind us that according to traditional philosophy the deep structure of the cosmos is a fluid opposition between *yin* 陰 and *yang* 陽, the two complementary forces shaping the *qi* 氣, or "material energy," of the universe into phenomenal reality. This means that the poetic practice of composing a Chinese sonnet—arranging sounds that resonate with that deep structure—is a literary means of bringing oneself into alignment with the ideal balance of the rest of the universe. Yeah, poetry is serious business. But we're using ☺ to remind us that poetry pleases (even when it's sad).

In English poetry, the metrical patterning takes place within a single line, horizontally: "Shall *I* com*pare* thee *to* a *sum*mer's *day*?" But in Chinese poetry, the metrical patterning takes place *between* the two lines of a couplet, vertically, we might say, like this:

The tone of every character must be the opposite of its (vertical) pair within a couplet. That means that all couplets, even those that are not semantically parallel, maintain a tonal balance of *yin* and *yang*. (I know, right?) But, strictly speaking, only the 2nd and 4th characters must do this; the rules allow for flexibility in the 1st and 3rd character positions if the poet wishes. Li Bai does this twice: character #3 of the chin couplet (☯/☯) and character #1 of the tail couplet (☺/☺).

This was the hot new style of court poetry in the seventh century, which had recently evolved out of Sanskrit prosody, and so it was called "recent-style poetry" 近體詩. It's silly we still call it that, but then the oldest bridge in Paris is still called *Le Pont Neuf, n'est-ce pas?*

There's also an intralinear metrical scheme, beginning here with a 3 + 2 pattern (☺☺☺+☻☻), followed by a couplet beginning on the opposite tone (☻☻☻+☺☺), which allows adjacent couplets to "stick" 粘 together via characters of the same tone in the 2nd and 4th positions (see "|" on the chart). It all snaps together like a Tang Lego® set. (*Li Bai action figure not included.*) We've already learned that there is only one rhyme, but there's more: It can only be a level tone. But our rhyme words are *chéng* 城, *zhēng* 征, *qíng* 情, *míng* 鳴: two rhymes, two tones. So, what gives? Well, in MC they sounded like *dzyeing, tsyeing, dzeing, meing*: one rhyme, all level ☺. In Cantonese, the rhymes still work (though the tones are off): *sing, tsing, tsʰing, ming*. If you speak only Mandarin like me, it kinda sucks (☹) to learn that Tang poetry sounded more like Cantonese. But in all dialects (☺) it still sounds beautiful (☻).

24

"Seeing Off a Friend," Jonathan Stalling

greēn	peāks /	cróss	nŏrth	wāll
whíte	streăms /	wìnd	eāst	tówn
ŏnce	wè /	pàrt	thís	pláce
mīles	páss /	weèds	rŏll	roūnd
cloúds	floát /	nó-	măds	moòd
òld	frìends /	feèl	sún	dówn
frōm	hĕre /	wàve	hānds	pàrt
neīgh	neīgh /	strāy	hŏrse	sóund

—JONATHAN STALLING (1997/2013)

The German Enlightenment philosopher Friedrich Schleiermacher (1768–1834) memorably observed that all translators have only two choices: leave the reader in peace and drag the author closer or leave the author in peace and drag the reader closer. Jonathan Stalling drags us as far into Chinese regulated verse as you can get in English.

We all know that part of what distinguishes poetry from prose is its emphasis on aural effects like rhyme, rhythm, assonance, alliteration, and the like. "The sound must seem an echo to the sense," as Mr. Pope put it in the early Qing dynasty. Replicating those aural effects in translation is crazy hard to do. At best, the typical thinking goes, you might create a roughly comparable effect among a new set of words however different from those of the original. Waley, for example, approximated Chinese pentasyllabics with a "sprung rhythm" borrowed from Gerard Manly Hopkins (1844–1889) with five strong accents per line (one per character) but otherwise no limit on unstressed syllables and no rhyme. The formal English versions we have seen so far do not mimic the Chinese form but use native English meters (iambic tetrameters and pentameters) and typical English rhyme schemes. All these translators drag the author a little closer to us.

Stalling does not. Growing up in a cabin in the Ozarks with parents who were back-to-the-land artists with an interest in Chinese philosophy, Stalling fell in love with Taijiquan, Tang poetry, and the Chinese language by the age of thirteen, went on to study Chinese art history at UC-Berkeley, and spent a year abroad at Peking University. He has since become a leading figure in interlingual experimental poetry and an influential speaker, editor, curator, and publisher. In 1997, while still an undergraduate, he was asked by the late great June Jordan (1936–2002) in a poetry class if he could convey in translation some of the word music of Tang poetry. His response was this poem, which he later published.

As he approached the task, Stalling set for himself "the same aural constraints as those followed in the original composition," that is, "a nearly monosyllabic lexicon with a set number of syllables per line" and a "strict end rhyme scheme." Strictly speaking, his rhyme scheme is ABCD-EBFD, but if we tell the truth slant, then *town, round, down, sound* all match the original scheme perfectly: AB-CB-DB-EB. (In modern Mandarin, by comparison, it's ABCB-DEFE.) He also decided to "mimic all cases of reduplicative binomes (repeated words) and other heightened acoustic textures." Hence, the *neīgh neīgh*. The results look something like a crib, but in fact only lines 1, 2, and 8 follow the original word order. Line 3, for example, which literally means something like "this place once do part" 此地一為別 becomes *ŏnce wè pàrt thís pláce*. Same rhythm and meaning but a slightly different word order. That's dragging the author at least a tiny bit closer to readers.

Stalling also decided to "compose the line with exactly the same tonal prosody" as the original, "with its harmonious alternation between *yin* and *yang* tones as pronounced in modern Mandarin." Thus, instead of "nativizing" or "domesticating" the tonal prosody of Chinese into the accentual-syllabic prosody of English (like Giles, Fletcher, Hart, and Xu), Stalling overlays the tone of each Chinese character onto the English word (or syllable) that occupies the same position in the original, thus "foreignizing" the meter into a form of Sino-English prosody. "Why modern Mandarin?" he asks. "Having cast off the metaphysical belief in a single 'original' song, it makes sense to mimic the poetry as it is recited today by the majority of Chinese people, not as it is imagined to have been recited during the Tang and Song dynasties." In other words, this is not meant to be some sort of onto-philological reconstruction of a Tang poem but a new mode of interlingual, conceptual poetry created by imitating the modern Chinese experience of a Tang poem. Creative imitation is a fundamental princi-ple of literary production. The only downside for the peace-loving reader is that you can't really read this hybrid poem unless you learn how to recite Tang poetry. And what's so bad about that? Stalling even places a slash (/) after the first two characters in each line to mark the caesura, where the Chinese reader typically pauses briefly during a recitation. I've heard Stalling recite this poem, and its evocation of the rhythm and lilt of the "original" is perfect.

One curiosity of this method is that every English word bears the tone of the character in that position regardless of its meaning. In line 3, for example, *pláce* does not bear the tone of *dì* 地 (place), because it stands where *bié* 別 (part) is located in the original line. Moreover, the balancing of *yin* and *yang* is invisible and inaudible here, since the characters in the positions of *cróss*, *tówn*, *thís*, *páss*, *cloúds*, *floát*, *nó-*, *sún*, *dówn*, and *sóund* all have "rising" tones (☯) in modern Mandarin, but had level tones (☺) in MC. Linguistic en-tropy makes the cosmic balance harder to perceive, but it's there, in the deep structure of the verse.

25

"Seeing Off a Friend," Gregory Whincup

Green mountains
Lie across the northern outskirts
Of the city.
White water
Winds around the eastern
City wall.

Once we make our parting
Here in this place,
Like a solitary tumbleweed
You will go
Ten thousand miles.

Floating clouds
Are the thoughts of the wanderer.
Setting sun
Is the mood of his old friend.

With a wave of the hand
Now you go from here.
Your horse gives a whinny
As it departs.

—GREGORY WHINCUP (1987)

I admit to a special fondness for Gregory Whincup's book since it was the first book I ever bought on Chinese poetry when I started learning Chinese. I loved it because it has word-for-word cribs, so I could try my hand at translating Tang poetry before I could read classical Chinese, like other notable rascals. What I love about this poem now is how closely it follows the rhythm of the Chinese line. This not only gives it a lovely pacing but also drags the reader just a little closer to the author—and yet so peacefully we hardly notice.

But let's take notice. As we just saw in Stalling's poem, every pentasyllabic line in regulated verse has a caesura (‖) after the first two characters. But the caesura is not just a rhythmic division in the line; it is almost always also a syntactic division:

浮雲	‖	遊子意
drifting cloud		traveler's thought
落日	‖	故人情
setting sun		old friend's emotion

The caesura delineates the two parts of the sentence while forging a clear connection between them without the need for a verb. As we've seen, that connection is neither a simile nor a metaphor exactly but on a continuum between them. Whincup marks the caesura with a line break: *Floating clouds ‖ Are the thoughts of the wanderer. / Setting sun ‖ Is the mood of his old friend.* He adds verbs (*Are, Is*) for a less pidgin-holed English, but dropping the article before *Setting sun* is a little pidgin-pocked, in order to form a more perfect union of parallel terms.

Thus, the caesura in a typical pentasyllabic line creates a strong rhythm with a distinct 2 ‖ 3 syllabic pattern consisting of 2 beats, a pause, then 3 beats. Moreover, those last 3 beats also tend to subdivide syntactically into a 1+2 or 2+1 pattern, since two of the three characters often form a pair. (See the diagram in the box.) Note that Li Bai's two parallel couplets (head and neck) have different postcaesural patterns: (1+2) and (2+1). Note also that the "flowing" parallelism of the chin couplet invites internal variation: (1+1+1) and (2+1). It must be said that like any metrical analysis, an awareness of these patterns may not help you understand the poem any better (though it can sometimes help you decipher a difficult line): The point is to help you appreciate its fabrication and aural texture, like raising a magnifying glass to the brushstrokes of a Titian. Are such textures translatable?

I certainly believe the caesura is. Whincup nearly does it. In six of eight lines his line breaks fall perfectly on the caesura (though he does subdivide the line again three of those times). Bravissimo.

青山‖(橫+北郭)	2‖(1+2)	(head)
白水‖(繞+東城)	2‖(1+2)	
此地‖(一+為+別)	2‖(1+1+1)	(chin)
孤蓬‖(萬里+征)	2‖(2+1)	
浮雲‖(遊子+意)	2‖(2+1)	(neck)
落日‖(故人+情)	2‖(2+1)	
揮手‖(自茲+去)	2‖(2+1)	(tail)
蕭蕭‖(班馬+鳴)	2‖(2+1)	

26

"Farewell to a Friend," Edward Chang

Blue mountains
lie across the northern outskirts;
white water
circles around the eastern town.
Once we part
from this place,
a lone thistledown
will be on a thousand-mile journey.
A floating cloud is
what you want to be like;
the setting sun is how
your old friend feels.
A wave of the hand,
and we go our own way.
Whinny, whinny,
the horses neigh.

—EDWARD C. CHANG 張暢繁 (2007)

When Edward Chang, now in his eighties, retired as a psychology professor two decades ago, he began translating classical Chinese poetry and self-publishing books about it. He also began writing his own poems, for the first time in his life, and joined a poetry writing club (in Hong Kong, by correspondence), which taught him how to compose Chinese sonnets. He's published a collection of 306 of his own Chinese poems along with English translations. On top of that, since retiring he has translated all of Shakespeare's 154 sonnets into—not one—but two different Chinese verse forms and rendered one of them back into English. (What a mensch!) When I grow up, I want to be like Prof. Chang.

Like Whincup, Chang follows the rhythm of the caesura for his line breaks but does so even more precisely. The resulting simplicity and adherence to the original form is elegant. Chang shows that one doesn't have to go all Ezraloomis to write a good translation. The parallelism of the opening couplet is perfectly recreated across the first four lines: *blue/white, mountains/water, lie/circles, across/ around, the/the, northern/eastern, outskirts/town.* The very slight cost is that it is hard to imagine precisely how those *mountains lie across* those *outskirts.* Do we need a tunnel to get into town?

It's not at all clear whom the *lone thistledown* (nod to Herdan) is supposed to represent, but that ambiguity is true to the original. We have to figure it out on our own. The neck couplet divides the cloud and sun metaphors between the two friends, but the friend is a wannabe cloud (*what you want to be like*) because he hasn't launched his life as a drifter yet. Chang thus reads *yi* 意 (thoughts) as the desire to set off, as if writing from within that moment when the friend's travel is still a future action. Yet the poet's *qing* 情 (feelings) are manifested by the *setting sun* at that very moment. (The difference between the definite and indefinite articles makes *the setting sun* seem to be real and present but *a floating cloud* to be a theoretical hypothesis.)

A *wave of the hand* seems at first to mean that only one of the friends is waving, but then the *we* in the next line suggests that both friends do. Once again, the ambiguity is true to the original, though *we go our own way* sounds like parting because of irreconcilable differences. The last line of the original is so hard to translate closely, or even distantly. *Whinny, whinny* feels just a little flat to me. But then, there's just nothing in English to prepare us for the onomatopoeic reduplication of *xiao xiao* but nursery rhymes. Argh argh, the translator growls.

Most translators lay down a single slab of text without a hint that the Chinese sonnet is made of couplets, like a wheel of parmigiano served without a knife. Indeed, some translators (Payne, Lowell) are so clueless they break up the couplets, then scramble to reassemble the parts. When readers learn how to proceed couplet by couplet on their own (as you, Dear Reader, are now doing), it's not as important for translators to lend a hand. But for now, what if we added just three line spaces to Chang's version, like this:

> Blue mountains
> lie across the northern outskirts;
> white water
> circles around the eastern town.
>
> Once we part
> from this place,
> a lone thistledown
> will be on a thousand-mile journey.
>
> A floating cloud is
> what you want to be like;
> the setting sun is how
> your old friend feels.

A wave of the hand,
and we go our own way.
Whinny, whinny,
the horses neigh.

The words are the same, but what a difference. It groups the proper elements together, recreates the pacing of the original, and highlights the parallelism. *Vive la différence*!

27

"Seeing Off a Friend," Red Pine / Bill Porter

Dark hills stretch beyond the north rampart
clear water circles the city's east wall
from this place where farewell begins
a tumbleweed leaves on a thousand-mile journey
drifting clouds in a traveler's thoughts
the setting sun in an old friend's heart
as we wave and say goodbye
our parting horses neigh

—RED PINE / BILL PORTER (2003)

Bill Porter (1943–) is a prolific translator of Tang poetry and sacred texts in the Daoist and Chan 禪 (Zen) Buddhist traditions who uses the pen name Chi Song 赤松 (Red Pine), which he adapted from the name of a Taiwanese soda pop company in the 1970s (HeySong 黑松 "Black Pine"). He only later learned it was the name of a legendary Daoist immortal. The anecdote perfectly captures his combination of humility and audacity. (Translators need both.) A big kind man with a big white beard, Porter traveled among the hermits living in seclusion in the mountains of southern China and stunned even Chinese urbanites with his book about them.

Porter distinguishes his version by giving us *clear water*, as only Zotolli and Belpaire had done before him, but goes a step further with *dark hills*, which brilliantly avoids having only one color word standing out like a sore blue-green thumb. The resulting parallelism is perfect. He avoids inserting a pronoun with *from this place where farewell begins*, which also gives duration and gravity to the moment. Porter doesn't tell us who the *tumbleweed* is who *leaves on a thousand-mile journey*, but then Li Bai doesn't either, so the metaphorical mental work the line makes us do is exactly the same. Spare and effective. It does seem a little odd to me that the *drifting clouds* are <u>*in*</u> *the traveler's thoughts* and the *setting sun* is <u>*in*</u> *an old friend's heart*, which metaphorizes thought and emotion as internalized natural objects instead of presenting a landscape reflecting subjectivity, but I'd also defend it as a lyrical way of connecting these paired elements. Both friends *wave*, and both *say goodbye* instead of merely "departing"—which may be too much human speech at that moment, but the ending is as fluid as free verse gets.

In a footnote, Porter matter-of-factly says that Li Bai wrote this poem in Xuancheng 宣城, adding that the "Shuiyang river still circles what remains of the city's east wall." That flatly contradicts my idea that it was written in Nanyang, almost five hundred miles away. Uh-oh. Does it matter? Well, only if we think there is no pun on *Baishui* 白水 ("White"/Clear River). In fact, Porter's is a popular notion, and it may not be wrong. (The citizens of Xuancheng certainly believe it, or at least promote the idea for domestic tourism, which is not exactly the same thing.) It's true that Li Bai spent plenty of time in Xuancheng as well as Nanyang, parted with friends there, and wrote poems there. And its landscape reflects the poem perfectly: Mount Jingting 敬亭山 stands to the north of the old city, and the Shuiyang River 水陽江 does wind around its east side. The idea is also appealing because everybody knows Li Bai's famous "quatrain" 絕句 "Meditating Alone at Mount Jingting" 獨座敬亭山, where the mountain is a sentient being, a friend: "A flock of birds, high above, flies into the distance. / A single cloud, all alone, passes leisurely by. / We two never tire of gazing at each other: / There is only Mount Jingting [and I]!" 眾鳥高飛盡. 孤雲獨去閒, 相看兩不厭, 只有敬亭山.

But there's a rub. In Li Bai's fifty or so poems mentioning the river at Xuancheng, the water is only ever *bi* 碧 (blue/green) or *lü* 綠 (green), whereas Nanyang's is consistently *bai* 白 (clear, bright, white). Moreover, another of Li Bai's sending-off sonnets shares some of the same diction. (See the box.) This poem pairs "old friend" 故人 with "traveler" 游子, just like our poem, and begins the final couplet with the same "wave" 揮手. Coincidence? Maybe. Might they have been written at the same time and place? Note how *old friend* and *traveler* refer to the same person here but are divided between the two in our poem for greater dramatic effect. In yet another poem about "Traveling to the Clear Purling Source at Nanyang" 游南陽清泠泉, Li Bai writes: "The western glow chases the flowing water, / rippling the *traveler's feelings*" 西輝逐流水，蕩漾游子情. As the traveler in this case, Li Bai is not venturing very far, but those sunset feelings by the river sound very familiar.

Seeing Off a Guest at Nanyang

Ladles of wine will not be spared
nor the smallest of honors neglected.

With deep regret
　　　　an *old friend* departs.
At unfair orders
　　　　the *traveler* grieves.

Sad faces
　　　　complain to the fragrant grasses.
Spring thoughts
　　　　entwine with the drooping willow.

[We] *wave* goodbye again and again,
helplessly mourning this parting of ways.

南陽送客

斗酒勿爲薄，　寸心貴不忘。
坐惜故人去，　偏令遊子傷。
離顏怨芳草，　春思結垂楊。
揮手再三別，　臨岐空斷腸。

28

Yinsong: In Song

｜郭 ！北 -橫 一山 -青
！別 一為 ！一 ｜地 ｜此
一征 ｜里 一萬 一蓬 -孤
｜意 ｜子 -遊 ｜雲 -浮
一情 ｜人 一故 ！日 ！落
｜去 一茲 ｜自 ｜手 -揮
一鳴 ｜馬 -班 一蕭 -蕭

｜城 一東 一繞 ｜水 ！白

We've seen how the caesura creates a basic rhythm for reci-
tation, a limping waltz of 1-2 *beat* 1-2-3. If the verse is hep-
tasyllabic (seven characters) instead of pentasyllabic (five
characters), poets shuffle their feet one more time at the
outset of each line: 1-2 1-2 *beat* 1-2-3. Otherwise, the meter
is exactly the same. During recitation, this rhythm lends a
songlike quality to the verse.

One of the earliest statements we have about Chinese
poetry comes from the *Book of Documents* 書經 some three
millennia ago: "Poetry gives words to thoughts. Song sings
those words forever" 詩言志歌詠言. Ancient poetry was
sung. Indeed, the ancient *Classic of Poetry* 詩經 is some-
times known as the *Book of Odes* or *Songs* since it contains
lyrics adapted from folk songs dating back some 12,000 years.
Of course, there are many kinds of Chinese poetry, some
more lyrical than others, but there is ample evidence that
the sonnet was also sung—or intoned or chanted—from the
Tang dynasty all the way up through the end of the Qing
dynasty in the early twentieth century. But what, exactly,
did it sound like?

Well, there's a group of enthusiasts who think they know.
Proponents of a growing movement in recent years have tried
to reconstruct and restore the art of "chanting" poetry, called
yinsong 吟誦, which they define in opposition to the merely
rhythmical *langsong* 朗誦 "reciting," which I've been de-
scribing so far. It's fair to say that some experts of classical lit-
erature are a little dubious about some of the specific claims
of these proponents. But even if their modern reconstruc-
tions of the rules for chanting do not precisely reflect histori-
cal practices—which must have varied from region to region
and century to century anyway—nevertheless, at least some
of the principles may be similar to what poets once used.

Scholarly skepticism hardly matters, however, to a
movement that has already gone totally viral, with regional

competitions attracting thousands of contestants and young
people chanting their favorite classical poems on TikTok to
millions of views. In 2019, *China Daily* reported that 100,000
elementary to high school teachers had already received
training in the method for classroom use. Part of the suc-
cess of the movement is surely that it bears a strong element
of national pride by evoking a cultural history thousands of
years old. Culture segments on the official China Central
Television channel show bands of schoolchildren in antique
garb chanting classical poetry in unison to the alternately
rousing and swooning accompaniment of traditional instru-
ments like the *qin* and *erhu*. And it's fun! It aids memoriza-
tion. And, for foreign students, it is always helpful to be re-
minded that Chinese poetry follows the ear, not the eye. Its
foundation is musical, aural, and vocal, not "ideographic,"
as centuries of Western linguistic fantasies would have you
believe.

The movement's most visible leader is a scholar named
Xu Jianshun 徐建顺 (1969–), who has worked closely with
nonagenarian scholars like Zhou Youguang 周有光 (1906–
2017) and Ye Jiaying 叶嘉莹 (1924–), who learned to chant
poems in their youth from aged scholars who had learned
the technique in the nineteenth century, purportedly pass-
ing down a tradition that had been interrupted by the West-
ern influence of "reciting" poetry instead of "chanting" it.
Proponents like Xu like to point out that musical notations
for chanting poetry like those you see here date back a thou-
sand years, although they appear only in texts preserved in
Japan and Korea, written by scholars who traveled to China
and came home with study notes. Oddly, there are no manu-
als or discussions of chanting techniques in Chinese. Xu is
quick to explain that the reason for this lack of textual evi-
dence is that nobody in China needed to write down what
everybody already knew how to do.

The notation system used here was adapted from those texts in Japan and Korea, then gradually refined and simplified in recent years along with the rules for chanting. The precise notes to be sung are up to the chanter—and of course the pronunciation will vary depending on the dialect—but certain rules are meant to apply to all *yinsong* performances. Chanting is based on meter.

Recall that in classical prosody, there are two tone categories: our friends, the *ping* 平☺ and the *ze* 仄☯. The most basic principle of *yinsong* is "*ping* low, *ze* high" 平低仄高. This means that characters in the *ping* ☺ class are sung in a lower pitch (marked with horizontal lines), and those in the *ze* ☯ class are sung in a higher pitch (marked with vertical lines). The vertical lines stand higher than the horizontal lines to remind us to chant them thus. The two tonal classes are thus clearly distinguished while leaving plenty of freedom for personal expression.

The remaining rules apply to duration, or how long you hold each syllable. Duration for *ping* ☺ characters will vary according to their position in the line:

A. *ping* ☺ in positions 1 and 3 is shortest (-)
B. *ping* ☺ in positions 2 and 4 is twice as long (--)
C. *ping* ☺ in a rhyme position is slightly longer (---)

The duration for *ze* ☯ (|) characters is always short, the same as the shortest *ping* ☺ above (-). The only exception is the very important *rusheng* 入聲 (entering tone), which is a subset of the *ze* ☯ class. (If you recall this from our earlier discussion of tonal meter, you may be a fellow nerd.) Xu explains that the exclamation mark (!) was chosen for this special tone for three reasons. First, its vertical line reminds us that the tone belongs to the *ze* ☯ class, but the dot at the bottom distinguishes it. (Henceforth, I shall use the notation *rusheng* ☯! for this special class mostly because it tickles my fancy.) Second, the "!" appears on all keyboards, so it's practical. And, third, characters in the *rusheng* ☯! (woo hoo) class in many dialects, such as Cantonese, always end with an unvoiced consonant (*-p*, *-t*, or *-k*), which gives the syllable a sharp and short sound (like an exclamation). Even though Mandarin lacks this ending, the chanting of these *rusheng* ☯! characters should be "short and strong" 短而重.

All of this is even trickier than it already looks, however, because the tone classes that dictate how a poem is to be chanted are the *ancient* tone classes used for the original compositions, which are not the same as modern tone classes. That means, even if you speak Chinese fluently, you can't just scan a poem for chanting according to what it sounds like now. It's even harder if you are doing it in Mandarin; Cantonese speakers still have the *rusheng* ☯! (woo hoo) to guide them, but Mandarin speakers will be completely at a loss. You need to learn the old tone categories for every word. And that's what the enthusiasts do.

Tang poems chanted with the reconstructed *yinsong* method can be beautiful and emotionally expressive but difficult to understand. As we've seen, classical poetry is dense and elliptical, nothing like modern speech. It's hard to follow even when recited clearly, to say nothing of when it is sophisticated with the musical intonation of *yinsong*. Most *yinsong* performances, however, draw from the repertory of classic poems that are commonly memorized by Chinese students as part of their education anyway, so we appreciate them like "covers" of big hits instead of novel expressions of meaning. Sound may prevail over sense, but the sense is already settled.

And yet, it turns out, sense is still in play. The proponents of *yinsong* like to say that you can't fully understand a well-made poem until you learn how to chant it. Chanting is said to reveal subtle meanings and poetic effects in the originals that mere reciters overlook. This stance presumes an interest in the fixed and essential meaning of certain sounds. (Indeed, *phonaesthemes*, as they are called, have received renewed interest from linguists in recent years, suggesting that certain sound clusters may carry specific associations, but chanting proponents tend to be more impressionistic than statistical.) So, for example, according to Xu, the rhyme category called *geng* 庚—which is the rhyme used in our poem—suggests a feeling of deep and lasting sincerity 庚韻 . . . 比較深遠真切. Because it does. Well, it also rhymes with *cheng* 誠 (sincere). Every poem using that rhyme presumably carries the same connotation, except for those that don't.

Here's an example of the sort of reading *yinsong* proponents like to do. In a typical recitation of line three, we would say:

this 此 place 地, [*pause*] once 一 make 為 separation 別

But if we were chanting the line, we'd say:

| | | ! | -- | |

this 此　place 地,　once 一　make 為 [*hold*]　separation 別

In the recitation style, the pause falls at the conventional caesura after *place* 地. But in the chanting style, even though there will also be a slight pause at the same spot, there will be a more pronounced delay holding the note after *make* 為, like a *fermata* in music. That's because *make* 為 has two beats (--) and follows the clipped *rusheng* ☯! word *once* 一, which takes a mere fraction of a beat, and the remaining *ze* ☯ words (|) all carry one beat (-). Thus, what a chanter might say (which the mere reciter of the poem purportedly would miss) is that Li Bai poignantly prolongs the moment of "making separation" or "completing the farewell" in the musical chanting of the line. After all, compared with a

simple *yi bie* 一別 (once separate), the addition of that ut-
terly unnecessary auxiliary verb *wei* 為 (make) has the effect
of delaying the inevitable moment of parting with just a
little more empty language, just a few more words between
friends with too little time and too much to say, which can
only be expressed "beyond the words" 言外.

29

"Seeing Off a Friend,"
Timothy Billings

The blue green mountains
        stretch out beyond the northern ramparts.
The clear White River
        bends around the eastern city wall.

This is the place where, once we finally part,
a lone bush will tumble away forever.

A drifting cloud,
        a traveler's thoughts.
A setting sun,
        an old friend's feelings.

From here, you set off with a final wave.
Bewildered, our horses whinny and sough.

—TIMOTHY BILLINGS (2024)

What Is He Doing?

Billings, like a few great translators—and not a few fairly unremarkable ones—is a failed poet who finds solace in translating the poetry of others. He's got a bee in his bonnet about parallelism. It's been quietly buzzing around in there since the early 1990s, when he studied Tang poetry in grad school with the formidable Mei Tsu-lin 梅祖麟 at the same time he was studying Shakespeare with the formidable Scott McMillin. (*Buzz, buzz. Words, words, words.* So Hamlet says.) He studied modern and classical Chinese at the ICLP in Taipei, earned an MFA in poetry and a PhD in early modern English literature at Cornell, as well as an MA in sinology at SOAS. After much buzzing and many words, he developed a translation method for the Chinese sonnet with a unique emphasis on parallelism. It has three chief features.

First, it divides the poem into couplet-stanzas so that readers can feel their way along its vertebrae instead of cracking the chin bone and connecting half to the head bone and half to the neck bone, as some unwitting translators have done. (Disconnect dem bones!) Second, it divides the lines of parallel couplets into two staggered hemistiches to distinguish them at a glance from the nonparallel couplets and to make their paired terms more salient. Third, and most importantly, it recreates the verbal parallelism in English as strictly as possible—or at least as strictly as lyrical diction and syntax will allow—so that readers can experience some of its rhetorical force and beauty. (*Oofda!* 噫吁嚱! So Li Bai says.)

In *The Literary Mind and the Carving of Dragons* 文心雕龍, a foundational work of Chinese literary criticism dating to about two centuries before Li Bai's sonnet, Liu Xie 劉勰 (c. 460–530) writes:

When Nature bestows form, limbs are always in
pairs. When the divine principle is realized, nothing
stands alone. Thus, when the mind creates liter-
ary language, it brings order to countless thoughts;
the high and the low must come together, naturally
becoming parallel.

造化賦形, 支體必雙, 神理為用, 事不孤立。
夫心生文辭, 運裁百慮, 高下相須, 自然成對。

Drop the mic. Parallelism may look like a highly artificial
linguistic constraint, but it derives from a transcendent
principle of nature. Low balances high. Left balances right.
And *yin* 陰 balances *yang* 陽. The bilateral symmetry of the
parallel couplet mirrors the whole of the animal kingdom
and manifests the metaphysical complementarity at the
heart of the cosmos itself.

Liu goes on to compare parallelism to the pendants of
fine jade that courtiers wore suspended from their belts,
usually in pairs, which clinked together musically as they
walked. He ends the chapter with these verses:

體植必兩	When bodies develop, they must be doubled.
辭動有配	When phrases proceed, they do so in pairs.
左提右挈	The left lifts. The right raises.
精味兼載	Essence and feeling are both conveyed.
炳爍聯華	Brilliant and dazzling, coupled flowers.
鏡靜含態	A mirror serenely holding an image.
玉潤雙流	Glistening jade in tandem flows
如彼珩佩	like matching jeweled pendants.

(Can you hear the hepcats snapping, each to each?)

And yet, for all that, in over a century and a half, vanishingly few translators have ever deliberately and consistently attempted to reproduce parallelism in English or any other European language. It's true that some specialists of Chinese literature do reproduce it when translating poems in scholarly discussions, but most translators of popular collections have been at pains to smother it, bend it, break it into unrecognizable pieces in favor of a less constrained aesthetic. (Some clearly never even recognized it in the first place, as we have seen.) The unfortunate result is that most readers who know Chinese poetry only through translation have no idea that such a distinctive aesthetic lies in the very marrow of its bones, despite innumerable introductions devoted to explaining it. (Readers of poetry books, I've discovered, tend to skip over the nerdy bits at the front.)

The gospel of this little book is intended for lovers of poetry who are new to Chinese. Nothing here is new to scholars of Chinese literature, who have been tilling this field for a long time. Back in the 1970s, two such specialists, the late Princeton sinologist Kao Yu-kung 高友工 (1929–2016) and the formidable Prof. Mei, collaborated on two major articles on the weediest weeds in Tang poetry, clocking in at over 150 bracing pages of analysis, which were published in the *Harvard Journal of Asiatic Studies*. Billings was playing little league baseball at about that time, but considering the influence that Mei would later have on his thinking a couple decades later, let's dip a toe into an idea or two of theirs to see how it helps us understand the Chinese sonnet in general and Billings's version in particular. What we have so far called the "chatty" and the "parallel" Kao and Mei call the "propositional" and the "imagistic." Sorry, but (with all due respect to the Martian) we're going to have to jargon the shit out of this.

By "propositional" they mean "that which appeals primarily to the understanding." Propositional language is discursive language. This includes claims, assertions, subjunctives, interrogatives, and imperatives. For Kao and Mei, the propositional involves a "truth claim," a statement that may be objectively true or false but that in any case reflects the subjectivity of the poet (when they "speak their truth," as we say). As such, in their view, a proposition "precipitates a fissure between the real and the imagery" insofar as we are aware that what we are told is subjective—not strictly or necessarily "real" but rather an assertion of the speaker—even when expressed with "imagery" that we might otherwise take to be a representation of objective reality. *This is the place where, once we finally part, / a lone bush will tumble away forever.* We see the bush tumbling away—and, of course, we know that tumbleweeds are real—but the statement is subjective, conjectural, propositional. Such utterances are explicitly or implicitly acts of *telling.*

By contrast, Kao and Mei call parallel couplets "imagistic." The term reminds us that this is where we find the highest density of imagery in a sonnet, but more importantly, Kao and Mei suggest that the distinct structure of parallel couplets often gives their imagery a different relation to reality, a fusion of phenomenology and ontology: "In the imagistic part of a poem, dream and fantasy merge into reality and the question of truth and falsity simply does not arise." The question is not whether *drifting clouds* really and truly "are" *a traveler's thoughts* or the *setting sun* really and truly "is" *an old friend's feelings.* Such statements are "true" and therefore "real" by virtue of their parallel syntax and framing—and also a healthy dollop of convention. In short, propositional couplets have "air quotes" around them, whereas imagistic couplets "merge into reality." (*Let be be finale of seem.* So the only Emperor says.)

Kao and Mei also characterize this difference as "perceptual" and "conceptual." The propositional presents *what is perceived*, while the imagistic presents a *conception of reality* that is incontrovertibly real, at least for the poem. (Not necessarily IRL.) Thus, while it is heuristically convenient to speak of the "objectivity" of imagistic couplets in order to distinguish their mode of representation from the "subjectivity" of propositional couplets, that so-called objectivity is nevertheless founded on a subjective experience—one that is "real" to the subject who experiences and expresses it in a poem and to us if we are reading it the way Kao and Mei say we should. (Of course, poets sometimes simply make stuff up, but that stuff is presumed to reflect the Real and True and to be experienced as such, unless it is satire.)

Kao and Mei identify other oppositions. Propositional couplets are "temporal," since they tend to narrate, moving forward or backward in time, whereas imagistic couplets are "spatial," since they seem to be frozen in time and to unfold in space. Moreover, propositional couplets are "continuous," flowing syntactically and logically (or at least along a single stream of thought), whereas imagistic couplets are "discontinuous." They like to strike camp in the middle of the quest and set up again in a different location.

Kao and Mei thus propose a list of qualities that structure the sonnet in oppositions that align with the two kinds of couplet:

PARALLEL	CHATTY
imagistic	propositional
objective	subjective
conceptual	perceptual
spatial	temporal
discontinuous	continuous

Of course, such binary schemes always eventually break down like every other two-wheeled chariot, but they can cover a lot of ground before they do. For Kao and Mei, this one illuminates how the sonnet progresses, which they see following a trajectory from the objective to the subjective, after the opening couplet:

> The middle couplets of Regulated Verse [for us, the Sonnet] are imagistic in language and discontinuous in rhythm; the final couplet is propositional in language and continuous in rhythm. The final line or couplet in Recent Style poetry often departs from the simple declarative mood; in which case its mood may be interrogative, hypothetical, exclamatory, or imperative; and its function in such moods is to speak the voice of the poet and to project the poem beyond its physical confines of four or eight lines. [Four lines in the case of a "quatrain" 絕句.] Time and place are usually indicated in the beginning of a poem, and as the poem progresses, the subjective mode generally supersedes the objective.

By now, all this should sound familiar. The surprise of horses vocalizing where we expect to find friends saying farewell is just such a subjective, nondeclarative utterance understood "to speak the voice of the poet" while kicking open the stable gate at the end of the poem to let the mind gallop off into the sunset lingering on the mountain tops. So also, time and place are established at the start of our poem, even though Li Bai's inversion of the first two couplets uses up one of his imagistic couplets in the setting of the scene, which in turn concentrates the true imagistic work of the poem into the neck couplet alone.

What comes next is a little boggy, but let's squish through it. For Kao and Mei (with a lone puff of Lacan in their sails), the final couplet serves another crucial function, which is the reunification of the poet-subject with the world: "The split between the Ego and the World is a traumatic experience that cries out for solace," which is supplied in the final couplet by propositional language that "mediates" that reunion so that "the poet not only sees the world, but sees himself, self-consciously, in the world; and this ego-centric turn, when compared with the purely objective mode of the imagistic part, gives the ending couplet a poignant personal tone." Thus, the exquisite vision of traveler and poet in the *drifting clouds* and *setting sun* is like an out-of-body experience in which Li Bai sees himself as part of the cosmos, after which his consciousness returns to his body, and he suddenly finds himself on horseback facing an old friend.

The solace provided by this ego-centric turn, however, is not to be confused with the merging of dreams and fantasy into reality that Kao and Mei attribute to the imagistic mode: "The primordial oneness of imagistic language should be distinguished from the reunification achieved through propositional language." We may be able to banter our way into Ego-World unification, but the Primordial Oneness that resides in parallel couplets is something profoundly different, an Ego-less merging with the World from which we must all eventually return to live our human lives.

Furthermore, for Kao and Mei, these structures have implications for translation, especially in imagistic couplets:

"Floating cloud, wandering son's mind" is one type of equivalence . . . in which the images remain strong and independent. But to say "floating cloud is like wandering son's mind" is to articulate discursively; it is to spell out the parts as parts and to indicate the relation between them, in this case, that of similarity. That the copula and simile-making verbs "is like,"

"seems"—the most conceptual of all verbs—occur
only in the ending couplet is another indication of
the division of labor between imagistic language and
propositional language in Recent Style poetry.

In other words, the moment we try to render the discon-
tinuous, paratactic phrases in an imagistic couplet into idi-
omatic, grammatical English, we are tipping the imagistic
into the propositional, changing lanes on autopilot, planting
hedges around the Primordial Oneness. Kao and Mei admit
that there is a "natural temptation" to do so but suggest that
"we should resist the temptation." Are *you* good at resisting
temptation? (Many a translator has not been.)

It's hard to disagree with Kao and Mei that there is a sliver of
daylight between a paratactic metaphor of pure juxtaposition
(clouds:thoughts) and a metaphor whose parts are leashed to-
gether with a copula (clouds *are* thoughts)—to say nothing
of a simile whose very natural-sounding expression (clouds
seem like thoughts) nevertheless has a guarded rationality to
it (clouds, after all, *are not* thoughts, even if they *seem like*
them in some situations), which puts us squarely in the propo-
sitional. The question for the translator is how important that
sliver of difference really is. At least one scholar, however,
Yan Zinan 顏子楠, a specialist in classical poetry at Beijing
Normal University, has provocatively challenged the view that
there is something essential and absolute about the parataxis
in imagistic couplets by suggesting that such verse almost al-
ways implies logical relations between the elements—like the
missing pronouns for verbs that Chinese readers supply by
convention—though he focuses on the more derivative po-
etry of the Song dynasty (immediately following the Tang),
where it is more common. In other words, there may be more
propositional "logic" in imagistic couplets than the prevailing
view of scholars like Kao and Mei would like to admit. What
a buzzkill.

What is at issue here is what we might call an equiva-
lence (or comparability) of *effect* in translation as opposed to
the ever-elusive equivalence of *meaning*. For Kao and Mei,
the goal of translation should be to reproduce the *effect* of
parataxis as closely as possible because of everything they at-
tribute to the function of imagistic couplets, and the way to do
that is by using parataxis in English. The assumption is that
parataxis works the same way in modern English as in me-
dieval Chinese (which may be true, or maybe not). In other
words, if two statements have the same (paratactic) form, will
they necessarily have the same function? At this point in the
discussion, I often find it useful to invoke Eugene Nida, the
controversial theorist of Bible translation for missionary use.
Nida distinguishes between "formal equivalence," a transla-
tion in the same form (i.e., word for word), from "functional
equivalence," in which the formal elements (from the order-
ing of terms to their very translation) might be altered to re-
produce a function that is equivalent to that of the original
text, whatever that might be. Nida, for example, says that the
functional equivalent for "white as snow" might be "white as
egret feathers" if you're translating into a language used by
people who live in a climate that has never seen snow—dif-
ferent words, same function. (I love how this idea forces us
to think about *meaning* as something created by context as
much as by individual words.) For Nida, of course, the func-
tion of scripture is to provide moral edification and spiritual
salvation, but for us, the function of a Tang couplet might
be the particular way it creates a literary or emotional effect.
Thus, if a paratactic utterance in classical Chinese is perfectly
grammatical and idiomatic, then (according to this view) an
English translation of it should also be perfectly grammatical
and idiomatic. How can a choppy line in English like "Setting
sun old friend emotion" truly represent what is actually a very
elegant line in classical Chinese? Form may follow function,
but function does not necessarily follow form. Is it even possi-

ble for an English sentence without a verb to be grammatical and idiomatic? Sometimes, surely.

Over the long last century, readers of poetry have gradually come to accept complete poetic utterances that previously would have been considered incoherent fragments of language. It took over a millennium, but European modernism finally arrived with an idiom for medieval Chinese poetry. Pound thought that he done it singlehandedly with his *Cathay* translations, but he merely placed the cornerstone around which others would build the ever-renovated edifice. The celebrated American poet David Young, for example, in the 1980s, achieves a lyrical economy in his translations unlike anything we've seen so far:

> one tumbleweed
> ten thousand miles to go
>
> high clouds
> wandering thoughts
>
> sunset
> old friendship

Young doesn't really read Chinese, but, dayum, dude knows how to write a poem in the modernest modernist idiom. In some sense, Young completes the project Pound started a century ago, also using his own cribs. He renders the imagistic parataxis without using an *is* or a *like*, and he does so with a lyricism that feels perfectly natural and familiar. (In the linguistic register of contemporary American poetry, these "fragments" are utterances both grammatical and idiomatic.) Kao and Mei would surely approve. But they would not likely be very happy about Young's dismantling of the poem's couplet structure to create (like Lowell and Payne) a wholly new structure of three equally isolated images in a row. Recall that the Chinese presents a single image in a propositional couplet (*This is the place where, once we finally part, / a lone bush will tumble away forever*), followed by two paralleled images in a very different sort of imagistic couplet (*clouds:thoughts::sun:feelings*). Young flattens out the difference.

The colon notation for analogies I just used may suggest a slightly different emphasis than the poem lays on these terms, but it does remind us that relations of comparison in a couplet are both horizontal and vertical: *Drifting clouds* [are like] *a traveler's thoughts* (horizontal) and also [are like] *the setting sun* (vertical). They are also potentially both analogous and oppositional: *Drifting* 浮 [is like] *setting* 落 insofar as they are both movements in space, but the first suggests upward movement and the second downward movement, etc. Note that in both of the previous two sentences, the colon indicates a rough equivalence between the two parts: What follows the colon restates the same idea in slightly different terms (just as this sentence does). That rough equivalence has suggested to some translators that the colon might be just what the Drs. Kao and Mei ordered.

One of those is the incomparable François Cheng 程抱一 (1929–). A poet, scholar, translator, novelist, essayist, and calligrapher, Cheng moved from China to Paris with his parents at the age of nineteen with no knowledge of French, then half a century later became the first person of Asian descent ever inducted into the Académie française—that singularly exclusive assembly dating back to the seventeenth century which can have only forty members at a time. (They're called *Les immortels*, but they do die, which is the only way for new members to join.) In his groundbreaking introduction to Tang poetry in the late 1970s, Cheng does it like this:

Nuage flottant: humeur du vagabond
Soleil mourant: appel du vieil ami

Floating cloud: mood of a wanderer
Dying sun: call of an old friend

A conjunction of elements without verbs or adverbs: just pure punctuation. Sweet. But the colon is still an interpolation into the system: Its presence has an organizing force, even if it is not a lexical one. The question is whether you prefer a graphic, nonvocalized interpolation or a vocalized one. For my part, I'm not sure. Often the colon seems to me to evoke discourses of logic, analysis, and explanation rather than poetic imagery: propositional punctuation colonizing the imagistic. (Prof. Yan might say this is inevitable.)

And yet the colon is precisely what Pound used in what is probably his best-known experiment with imagism, "In a Station of the Metro," well before he began working with Chinese cribs:

The apparition   of these faces   in the crowd:
Petals   on a wet,   black bough.

If I'm not mistaken, the colon functions here very much like François Cheng's. Just try replacing it with "are" and "are like" to hear the difference. [*This should be attempted only by trained scholars in a controlled environment.] The colon unequivocally establishes a metaphorical equivalence between the two parts.

It is therefore all the more interesting that Wai-lim Yip 葉維廉, who wrote a book-length study in admiration of Pound's versions in *Cathay*, does not follow Pound's lead here. Like Kao and Mei (and Cheng), Yip believes that "there is a flash of interest in the syntactically uncommitted resemblance which the introduction of the *verbs* (thus making it a metaphor) and the word *like* (thus making it a simile) destroys easily." But instead of using a colon to achieve that "syntactically uncommitted resemblance" (that phrase *is* rather nice, isn't it?), he chooses semicolons:

Floating clouds; a wanderer's mood.
Setting sun; an old friend's feeling. (1969)

In a later revision, his semicolons are reduced to commas:

Floating clouds, a wanderer's mood.
Setting sun, an old friend's feeling. (1976)

I doubt that anyone could make an argument in favor of either of these that is not primarily rooted in personal preference. To me, the semicolon often feels formal and serious; the comma feels light and easy. But formality and seriousness are not necessarily contrary to the letter and spirit of a Chinese sonnet.

In 1971, the justly famed translator Burton Watson dashed through the parataxis (as Xu Yuanchong would later do):

Drifting clouds—a traveler's will;
Setting sun—an old friend's heart.

But who's to say—save Emily Dickinson, perhaps—that this is the best of the lot? Perhaps if there were a preexisting literary convention for representing the caesura in an English line, we could use that to bridge the gap where the caesura conventionally falls in a Chinese line, but we lost the caesura when we lost Anglo-Saxon alliterative verse. (Indeed, some translations of Old English poetry use a gap of several spaces to bridge the gap of several centuries.) In our poem, it might look like this, using Watson's diction:

Drifting clouds   a traveler's will;
Setting sun   an old friend's heart.

That works. The only question in my mind is how seamlessly that style would fit into the rest of a translation and whether it would look odd and unnecessary in other sonnets where the imagistic couplets *do* contain verbs. What if we just ran it all together without punctuation or special typography of any kind, leaning into the formal equivalence?

> drifting clouds a traveler's will
> setting sun an old friend's heart

That really requires the reader to step up—and it's hard not to read the plural *clouds* as a verb, though the singular *sun* doesn't work the same way for a parallel. Now there's a thought. Could that be exploited with the gerunds already there?

> clouds drifting a traveler's will
> sun setting an old friend's heart

Yowza. A martini with a twist. You could build a poem around that, if you had the nerve. But my point is still the same, that choosing among the various possibilities created by this couplet is extremely difficult and mostly a matter of personal taste.

What He Did

With all this in mind, let's now critique Billings's translation, measure for measure, as he has done for others. *The blue green mountains / stretch out beyond the northern ramparts. // The clear White River / bends around the eastern city wall.* To begin, Billings throws all his noodles against the city wall to see what sticks: His *blue* conjures an image of distant mountains in low light (*cum* Pound et al.), while *green* evokes what most readers of Chinese will see. Can he not decide? (Is he a Libra?) At least he doesn't settle on a single word for a blended color like cyan, cerulean, azure, aqua, teal, turquoise, or "alcedine"—the last of which derives from the Latin word for the kingfisher, whose stunningly iridescent blue-green-purple-black feathers notoriously prompted the philologically zealous sinologist Peter Boodberg to recommend it as the preferred translation for *qing* 青. At least there's that. Using two color words also allows

Billings to use two for *bai* 白 in the next line while preserving his precious parallelism, so that he can use a capitalized *White* for the proper name of the river (well, he couldn't drop that after making such a fuss about it, could he?), while at the same time clarifying that it really means *clear*, though that's not really a color word, is it? It almost works. Only the sense of "bright" is missing. Earlier, Billings admired how Red Pine skirts this conundrum of polysemous color words by simply pairing *dark* with *clear* (though "bright" might make a better parallel), but he's too much of a philological busybody to follow. What if he had used three words for each Chinese color word in order to include all potential meanings? "The dark, blue green mountains/stretch out beyond the northern ramparts.//The bright, clear White River/bends around the eastern city walls." Nah, too many noodles.

Billings's translations of pentasyllabic lines often perfectly replicate the original 2 ‖ 3 syllabic pattern with 2-beat and 3-beat hemistiches, but he's got way too much going on in this couplet to pull that off. As for his pet parallelism, note how he matches even the articles (*The blue green*, *The clear White*), even though "blue" alone would be a slightly more lyrical attack for the line ("Blue green mountains"). But since he can't dispense with the article before the proper name of the river, he won't drop the article before *blue green*. (He also might have used the singular "a" *blue green* mountain—since there is that Lone Mountain 獨山 immediately north of Nanyang— but, apparently, he couldn't commit to it.) The drive for such perfect symmetry looks a little obsessive, almost compulsive, one might say. (*Everybody's got a thang*. So Mr. Wonder says.) Some lyricism is undoubtedly sacrificed for semantic richness and formal symmetry (the Faustian pact of the philological translator), but not all of it. Head couplet? A–/B+

(Extra credit for the staggered hemistiches.)

This is the place where, once we finally part, / a lone bush will tumble away forever. After the soberly mouthed rhythm of the head couplet, the chin-wagging chin couplet rolls trippingly off the tongue. Earlier, Billings had acknowledged the "flowing water parallelism" 流水對 of this couplet, but he presents it here without hemistiches because of its manifestly propositional feel and function. (Typographically distinguishing between parallel and nonparallel couplets may occasionally force a hard distinction that might otherwise remain somewhat fluid in the original, but such an occasional loss of subtle formal ambiguity is far outweighed by the attention it draws to genuine distinctions that are consistently lost in all other translation methods anyway.) Where Pound awkwardly calques *wei bie* 為別 as "make separation," Billings gives us *finally part* to recreate how the empty, semantic redundancy in the Chinese phrase seems to draw out the length of the line, as if putting off the moment of parting. The result is also a perfect iambic pentameter line, with one extrametrical syllable in "finally" (depending on how you say it), which is thematically resonant with delay: *Thīs is the pláce where, ōnce we finally párt.* (Nerd alert: The trochaic first foot is a standard variation, but then you knew that.) That metrical regularity, moreover, has the effect of making the next line bump along even more like the tumbleweed it slyly suggests without dragging us into the Wild Wild West: *a lōne būsh will tūmble awāy forēver.* (OK, OK, so he studied some poetry, MFA and all that, for better or for worse.) Like Obata, Billings renders the awkwardly hyperbolic distance as time (10k "miles" to *forever*). Technically, the place *where* should be "*from* where," or even "from which" (the *lone bush will tumble*), since the suggestion now is that it will be tumbling in this one place forever— but Billings seems to think most readers won't stumble over that, and greater precision would ruin the rhythm, as follows

(WARNING: ASK YOUR DOCTOR BEFORE READING THIS LINE. SIDE EFFECTS MAY INCLUDE DIZZINESS AND NAUSEA.): "This is the place from which once we finally part." Philology? TKO. This round goes to Lyricism. Chin couplet? A/A–

And now we arrive at the imagistic neck couplet, so called because it throttles every translator who approaches it. The nerdiest scholars, in essays known as "poetry chats" 詩話 beginning in the Song dynasty, liked to talk about the "poem's eye" 詩眼. (Think hurricane, not Cyclops.) It's what Pound would have called the *vortex* or "point of maximum energy." It could be a couplet, a line, or even a single word or phrase, sometimes more narrowly called the "eye-word" 字眼. As you should be able to guess by now, the eye of this poem is the neck couplet; the eye-words, *drifting cloud(s)* 浮雲 and *setting sun* 落日. Usually, the eye-word is a verb, but not here, since, as you know, this couplet has no verbs. (And thereby hangs a tail fit to make a fly whisk.) Drum roll, please . . .

A drifting cloud, / a traveler's thoughts. // A setting sun, / an old friend's feelings. Commas? Are you kidding me? After such a bother over every conceivable option for the parataxis in this couplet, Billings settles on *commas*? I don't know about you, but I was expecting something revolutionary. Periods, maybe?

A drifting cloud.
　　　A traveler's thoughts.
A setting sun.
　　　An old friend's feelings.

Simple, graphically elegant, verifiably novel. Now we're talkin'. The visible and abstract elements flash upon the imagination in turn, separated yet proximate in a way that demands some sort of cognitive fusion. And yet, as we've already stressed—and it can't be stressed enough—this may be nothing more than a matter of taste. But if we had to guess why Billings didn't go for periods, well, we could just say he's gutless. Or we could say that the separation of elements would be too absolute, whereas the comma functions more like the caesura in the Chinese line, binding together the paratactic elements while also maintaining their discreteness. Moreover, one function of the comma is to introduce an equivalence, a reiteration for clarity, a definition riding shotgun, a sort of casual colon, an equal sign lite—one that is less conspicuous than a dash—in "appositive phrases" like the ones in this sentence. Billings also tends to reserve periods for lines that contain multiple subject-predicate statements, which occur more frequently in the longer lines of heptasyllabic verse, such as the famous opening line: "The moon sets. Crows caw. Frost fills the sky" 月落烏啼霜滿天. It's just how he does it.

Combined with the commas, the staggered hemistiches really shine in this neck couplet, as Billings can't quite pull off in the head couplet: That extra measure of separation forces us to pause just a little more when reading, which helps us navigate the dense fog of the parataxis. Billings joins the minority in favoring the singular *cloud* over the plural (along with Pound, Zottoli, Forke, Xu Yuangzhong, Gilonis, and Chang). That may have as much to do with maintaining the parallelism among the other single terms (*cloud, traveler, sun, friend*) as it does with the beauty or appropriateness of a solitary cloud, like a solitary tumbleweed, to describe the solitary traveler. Of course, *sun* can only be singular. Shouldn't A *setting sun* be "The" *setting sun*? How many other suns are there? (What planet is Billings on?) We might say the indefinite article gives one the sense of looking out on the world like a painting—there's a cloud, there's a sun—which you might see differently on another occasion but which on this occasion has the particular richness and significance that the imagistic couplet manifests. Some days, there *is* no sun. One's subjective experience of the world on such melancholy, overcast days "merges with reality." If you believe Kao and Mei, it's what the imagistic mode does.

As for the opposition of *yi* 意 and *qing* 情, we've seen "will" and "heart" (Watson), "thoughts" and "heart" (Porter), "thoughts" and "longing" (Obata), *pensées* "thoughts" and *souvenir* "memory" (Belpaire), "dreams" and "affections" (Payne), "whim" and "sentiments" (Lin), "feeling" and "affection" (Xu Yuanchong), and "thoughts" and "mood" (Whincup). Only Gilonis, in his second experimental piece, uses "thoughts" and "feelings," as Billings does, though Herdan's "thoughts" and "emotions" comes close. Call it a lapse of imaginative powers, if you must, but you might also understand it as a willingness to allow the simple terms to relax in place and to beckon the reader closer, as they do in the Chinese, without feeling the need to pump up the volume with something more inventive or conspicuously lyrical. Watson's "heart" has genuine lyrical appeal, to be sure, but insofar as the material thing ought to be complemented with a subjective emotion (*sun:feelings*)—that is, a movement from the concrete to the abstract—"heart" confusingly introduces yet another material thing in a submetaphor within the metaphor (*sun:heart* [= *feelings*]), making it lean a little to one side. But that may be a problem only if parallelism is what matters most to you. So, for this exceptionally difficult couplet, Billings follows Yip's commas, in the end, but by adding the staggered hemistiches, he slows down the pace of reading at the caesurae, which helps us make sense of the parataxis. Neck couplet? A+ (☻)

From here, you set off with a final wave. Adding *final* before *wave* nicely fills out another iambic pentameter line, smoothly resuming the chatty flow once again, though it does suggest there may have been some previously unreported waving. Billings inverts the original syntax (which is: *wave* 揮 *hand* 手 *from* 自 *here* 兹 *go* 去) probably because "With a wave of your hand, you set off from here" just sounds like clumsy calquing. You go, Lyricism! Tail couplet, line one, subtotal? A

Bewildered, our horses whinny and sough. To be *bewildered* is to be lost and confused—etymologically, what happens if you should suddenly find yourself in the wilderness, separated from the comfort and safety of others. In that sense, it is just what a horse might feel in such a moment, a kind of distressed disorientation. Moreover, it recalls Li Bai's allusion to the Han-dynasty story of horses crying out during a nighttime battle when they become separated from one another. It's a bold choice, philology and lyricism hanging in the balance. The sheer novelty of it is seductive. (Could it be a darling to be killed off?) One potential downside to *bewildered* is that it may be more direct and explicit in its expression of feeling than the Chinese because it names a state of mind, whereas the Chinese is famously indirect. Yet there's no doubt that the onomatopoeic *xiao-xiao* 蕭蕭 combined with the verb *ming* 鳴 (cry out) gives the original Chinese line an unmistakably melancholy cast, one that is challenging to render lyrically in its entirety. No quack-quack, neigh-neigh here, of course; Billings learned that lesson the easy way. Instead, he uses two verbs for two different kinds of horse sound (made by *both* horses, by the way). As we've seen, translators sometimes get hung up on *xiao-xiao* 蕭蕭, as if the doubled characters in Chinese require a doubling in English. What they often don't realize is that onomatopoeia is always expressed in Chinese through what are called *diezi* 疊字 (reduplicated characters) or *dieyin* 疊音 (reduplicated sounds). The doubling itself isn't necessarily significant, certainly not literal. It's a linguistic convention. (In just such an unguarded moment, Young unfortunately ends his otherwise exquisite translation: "your horse / whinnies / twice.") Billings knows better than to snag his jeans on that barbed wire, so perhaps his double *whinnies and soughs* has more to do with resolving the rhythm of the line and with the different implications of the shrill "cry" 鳴 and the swishing of 蕭蕭. Together they suggest both the urgency of whinnying and the resignation of soughing, the distress of an unpleasant surprise and the grief of a definitive separation.

Final grade: A/A–

Nice work! (☺)

Epilogue
What's in a Name? The Sonnet

I have embraced the term "Chinese sonnet" for the *lüshi* 律詩, or "regulated verse poem," in order to give it local habitation and a name, though it does come with some baggage. Considering that Li Bai lived a thousand years before Shakespeare, it would make more sense to call Shakespeare's sonnets "English *lüshi*" (as I sometimes do, to annoy my students) instead of the other way around. But if the familiar can lead us to the rich and strange, one carry-on and one personal item are certainly allowable, so long as they are properly stowed after takeoff. Nobody (but Dogberry) really believes that comparisons are odorous, and the "regulated verse poem" smells just as sweet by any other name. I do not in any way wish to reduce it to the European sonnet but rather to draw as much attention to it as possible with this mildly provocative comparison (which better sinologists than I have made) especially for those who might otherwise be put off at first by a more unfamiliar or unwieldy term. Undoubtedly, critics will whinny and sough, but the training wheels can be taken off at any time, to pedal away on *lüshi* alone. My modest hope is that readers come away from this little book confident in their knowledge that Tang lyrics do *not* actually sound much like the poetry of Ezra Pound—or Louise Glück or James Wright, as much as I have admired them both. My hope is that the comparison may help others appreciate both verse forms better. And to that end, let's use this comparison for a final chariot charge, once more into the breach.

Although Shakespeare wrote some of his most beloved plays before the age of forty and died when only fifty-two, he is known in China (where age is traditionally venerated) by the honorific soubriquet Shaweng 莎翁 (Old Man Sha), not unlike the way some folks in English like to call him "the Bard," as if there were only one. Li Bai, for his part, is formally known as Taibai 太白 (Extremely Bright), which is his *zi* 字, or "courtesy name" (an adult name adopted about the age of twenty). Taibai is also the name in Chinese astrology for the planet we call Venus, as well as the name of a rainmaking deity in the Daoist pantheon. Legend has it that when Li Bai's mother was pregnant, she dreamed one night that Venus had fallen out of the sky and into her belly (we've heard that one before), and she believed her son might be a reincarnation of the god. Venereal influences notwithstanding, however, Li Bai did not become a writer of love poems like Shakespeare, and herein lies the first point of difference.

As some of the other nerds among us may already know, the English sonnet derived from the Italian *sonneto* (little song), which was made famous in the fourteenth century by Francesco Petrarca (1304–1374), who wrote over three hundred of them to a certain hottie he spotted in church one day called "Laura" (her name may have been changed to protect her innocence, but maybe not), who was faithfully married and, to put it nicely, not interested. The sonnet thus came to be associated with intense passion, rhetorical flattery, and frustrated desire, as well as with the power of poetry to grant eternal fame (in a tradition stretching back most notably to Virgil), since *sonneti*, it turned out, didn't actually get you laid. The first sonnets in English appeared in the early sixteenth century during the reign of Henry VIII, when court poets translated some of those *sonneti* using the same meter and rhyme scheme, then gradually adapted the form to better suit the relatively rhyme-poor nature of English, which is how Shakespeare found it at the end of that century.

The "Chinese sonnet" emerged in the sixth century in the courts of the great Southern states, owing its origin at least in part to the metrical theories of Shen Yue 沈約 (441–513), who was probably influenced by the tonal *śloka* meter of Buddhist *sūtras* written in Sanskrit, though some Chinese scholars continue to search for a purely "native" origin for this cultural treasure, probably in vain. By the eighth century, the ability to write a formally perfect sonnet was a requirement for the imperial examination leading to almost any government office. Although a small percentage of Chinese sonnets do qualify as love poems—Li Shangyin 李商隱 (813–858) is particularly noted for his—the Tang sonnet for the most part is devoted to nonamorous topics such as friendship and farewells, holidays and laments, encomia and political allegories, expressions of gratitude, and philosophical reflections on one's place in the human and nonhuman worlds. When Tang poets do write about love, they tend to focus on separation and nostalgic longing rather than on the agonies of desire, though figurative idealizations of the female body—the *blazon* so striking in Petrarch and his imitators—are also de rigueur when women are described, with hair like clouds, eyebrows like distant mountains or moths, and lard-white skin.

All sonnets, almost by definition, demand plenty of flashy verbal art, though in Chinese this is mostly concentrated in

the antithetical parallelism of the middle two couplets, as
we've seen. Petrarch also had a fondness for antitheses: "I fear
and I hope; I burn and I'm ice . . . /I grasp at nothing, and
I embrace all the world" (*e temo, et spero; et ardo, et son un
ghiaccio . . . /et nulla stringo, et tutto 'l mondo abbraccio*).
But whereas the European sonnet uses antithesis to express
destabilizing extremes of passion, the antithetical pairings in
Chinese parallelism create balanced oppositions in their evo-
cations of "scenes and emotions blended together" 情景交融.

As for rhyme, nothing jingles like the sound of like endings
(as Milton used to say), and Tang poets knew how to jingle.
Italian is a rhyme-rich language, so Petrarch could get away
with two rhymes in the 8-line "octave" beginning the poem
(ABBA-ABBA) and three or even only two rhymes in the 6-line
"sestet" closing it. That's only four or five rhymes in fourteen
lines. Since English is relatively rhyme-poor, Shakespeare
typically uses seven rhymes: ABAB-CDCD-EFEF-GG. The
Chinese sonnet, by comparison, is limited to a single rhyme,
stitching together all those otherwise self-contained couplets
into an exquisite balance of parts and whole: AB-CB-DB-EB.
That's because Chinese has oodles of rhyme words. In longer
verse forms, the rhyming can go and on and on, so much so
that Liu Xie 劉勰 at the turn of the sixth century suggested
that using the same rhyme a hundred times in a row might
not be the best idea because it is "laborious for the mouth and
lips to pronounce" 百句不遷則唇吻告勞.

As you may recall from the preceding pages, the Chi-
nese sonnet is actually an exemplar of the broader mode
of verse known in the Tang dynasty as "recent-style poetry"
近體詩, whose metrical foundation is the strict arrangement
of tones. (The other exemplar is the "quatrain" 絕句, which
is essentially half a sonnet, but that is the topic for another
book.) And yet, to make matters even more complicated, the
sonnet has even more restrictions than those we've covered

thus far: Shen Yue's metrical analyses eventually gave rise to the famous "Eight Defects" 八病, a list of internally clashing sound patterns to be avoided for the most mellifluous effects, some of which have such colorful names as "flat head" 平頭, "rising tail" 上尾, "wasp waist" 蜂腰, and "crane knees" 鶴膝. (Nerd out on all the juicy details in the notes, if you wish.) Li Bai was a maverick devoted to reviving the "old-style poetry" 古體詩, which had much looser metrical demands, but the roughly 120 sonnets and 80 quatrains that come down to us among his one thousand or so extant poems show he was also a master of metrical form. For his part, Shakespeare left us over 150 sonnets in a stunningly regular meter, despite a few deliberate variations on the form. Both of them make conforming to strict rules look much easier than it is.

The English sonnet and the Chinese sonnet are also strikingly similar in rhetorical structure, both containing a tripartite form superimposed with a quadripartite form. According to traditional Chinese criticism, a poem or essay ought to have four clearly delineated stages: (1) opening 起; (2) extending 承; (3) turning 轉; and (4) closing 合. Like this:

> Shall I compare thee to a summer's day? (起 open)
> Thou art more lovely and more temperate:
> Rough winds do shake the darling buds of May,
> And summer's lease hath all too short a date:
>
> Sometime too hot the eye of heaven shines, (承 extend)
> And often is his gold complexion dimmed;
> And every fair from fair sometime declines,
> By chance, or nature's changing course untrimmed:
>
> But thy eternal summer shall not fade, (轉 turn)
> Nor lose possession of that fair thou ow'st,

Nor shall death brag thou wander'st in his shade,
When in eternal lines to time thou grow'st:

So long as men can breathe or eyes can see, (合 close)
So long lives this, and this gives life to thee.

That's how it rolls: *qi* 起, open with a thought (you are more
beautiful and faithful than a summer's day); *cheng* 承, extend
that thought (indeed, a summer's day is flawed and fleeting
like all beauty); *zhuan* 轉, hang a left (*but*—here it comes—
your beauty is eternal and immortal); and *he* 合, close it up (all
because I wrote this poem for you). *Ars longa, vita brevis*, and
the rest is history. Shakespeare's sonnets can be dense and in-
timidating at first, but once you've read enough of them, they
have a predictable rhetorical structure that is not only reassur-
ing but also essential to the pleasure they offer, like bringing
a chord progression to its resolution. The same is true for the
Chinese sonnet. Internalizing that structure makes you a bet-
ter reader of the verse form and allows you to appreciate the
subtle effects when poets play within and against the form, as
the best inevitably do.

So, even though the English sonnet has four parts (three
quatrains and one couplet, or 4 > 4 > 4 > 2), the first two
quatrains often seem to combine into an 8-line block, since
they typically present and develop a single idea before the
sonnet makes its turn (*volta*), lending it the feel of three un-
equal movements narrowing steadily toward a pithy closure:
8 > 4 > 2. Similarly, among the four couplets of the Chinese
sonnet (2 > 2 > 2 > 2), the middle two couplets tend to stick
together because of their distinctive parallelism (and every-
thing that it entails), framed by more discursive opening and
closing couplets, like an image sandwich on two slices of
proposition: 2 > 4 > 2. That means, of course, that if you map
the prototypical *open-extend-turn-close* pattern evenly onto

the prototypical Chinese sonnet, couplet by couplet, then the "turn" 轉 will fall *between* the two parallel couplets in the middle of the poem. But how can there be a "turn" between two identically parallel couplets?

Well, the short answer is that they are *not* identically parallel. The immortal François Cheng has observed that a shift typically takes place between two imagistic couplets in both *content* and *syntax*. From one to the next, there is a shift in the semantic categories used for parallel terms, so that, for example, if colors and flowers and weather are used in one, the next might use numbers and implements and proper names. There is often also a shift of perspective, from past to present, for example, or from large to small, public to private, etc. And there is almost always a shift in the syntactical patterns, so that, for example, if the first couplet parses as

adj. + noun ‖ verb + adj. + noun,

the second might go

adj. + noun ‖ adj. + noun + verb.

Many of the rules for recent-style poetry are aimed at avoiding repetition, and such subtle variations as this can create a lilting feeling of free movement within the otherwise tight strictures of the form.

Cheng also observes that the temporal-spatial movement of the sonnet (from time to space then back to time) is typically nuanced with two modes—open and closed, static and dynamic—which include a shift from one parallel couplet to the next. He illustrates the idea with a diagram like this:

Couplet 1: closed time
{ Couplet 2: static space
{ Couplet 3: dynamic space } parallel couplets
Couplet 4: open time

This improved, four-wheeled chariot won't run perfectly in the ruts of every Tang sonnet, but you'd be surprised by how many it does. The "closed" time at the beginning of a sonnet is the poet's "lived time," according to Cheng, which the poet tries to surpass via "a spatial order" rediscovering some "intimate relationship with things" before falling back into what he calls the "exploded time" of the final couplet, which is "a time broken open and assured of further metamorphoses." (Can I just say? That is frickin' brilliant.) Ideally, that "exploded time" would evoke some thought or feeling "beyond the words" 言外, as if following what was not said in the direction of whatever changes must follow the poem's final moment. The subtle shift from "static" to "dynamic" space may sometimes be difficult to discern in some sonnets, especially if you are looking only at translations, but give it a try. Recall that our sonnet is a bit jumbled up, since the first and second couplets are sort of swapped, so our parallel couplets are really the first and third: a *static* landscape with mountains, a river, and a city; and a *dynamic* landscape of floating clouds and a falling sun in fluid relation with human emotions. For more typical examples near at hand, look again at the extra sonnets in Chapters 14 and 27.

Although our sonnet does not conform precisely to Cheng's ingenious schema, its novel rearrangement still follows the rhetorical structure we've been discussing, perhaps even more closely for that reason: couplet 1, *opening* 起 on a location (static space); couplet 2, *developing* 承 the prospect of parting in that location (closed time); couplet 3, *turning* 轉 to floating clouds and the setting sun, which suggests the thoughts and emotions of traveler and poet (dynamic space); then couplet 4, *closing* 合 with a wave, a departure, and the pathos of bewildered horses and the parting of friends (open time). In short, Li Bai's slight bending away from one formal convention bends toward another.

There is, of course, much more to learn about Tang poetry—from the impact of the devastating An Lushan rebellion (one of the deadliest conflicts in all human history) to the biographies of individual poets (both apocryphal and true), which inform our understanding of their poetry, along with a brave new world of allusions to grok. As I hardly need to say, you can learn only so much about the poetry of a culture or an era by looking at a single poem. (Imagine, if you will, a class of earnest college students in China studying English literature by reading a single Shakespearean sonnet translated into Chinese a couple dozen different ways. Yeah, maybe don't think about that right now.) One can get a good grip on the form this way but little else.

And yet let's not underestimate the power of poetic form.

As I close, I feel I must say that my emphasis on form in this little book is not in any way intended as a covert or naïve retrenchment into formalism per se in opposition to other indispensable critical approaches, each with its own demands, advantages, and urgencies—which inform my other critical writing and my teaching, as well. But since "form" as an epistemological framework is especially well suited for grasping the unfamiliar, it is an empowering place for beginners to begin. And this is a book (primarily) for beginners (of one kind or another). I hope it will embolden readers to seek out new discoveries in Chinese poetry. And let us not forget that the great Tang poets accepted this demanding, arbitrary, and artificial form as the stone in which they carved, the given medium in which some of their loveliest and most powerful aesthetic effects were wrought—that is, in the cunning organization of poetic language, rather than in the poetic language itself, if such a distinction can ever be made. This may not be exactly what Chinese poets mean when they speak of how the best poetry suggests meanings "beyond the words" 言外, but it is at least a source of literary pleasure—which is a real pleasure for a great many of us—in a world made less painful and more beautiful because of the collective efforts devoted to such ethereal dignities from century to century, which anyone with the will can share and which we need now as much as Li Bai ever did, over a thousand years ago.

And that's not a bad place to begin.

Acknowledgments

I would like to express my gratitude to the President and Board of Trustees of Middlebury College for the sabbatical leave during which I wrote the first draft of this book, and to the Andrew W. Mellon Foundation for the New Directions Fellowship, which allowed me to deepen my study of classical Chinese after having become a Shakespeare professor. It has been one of the greatest pleasures of my life.

Notes

Unless otherwise noted, all quotations from Li Bai's poetry are taken from Li (1977). Unless otherwise attributed, all translations are my own.

Introduction

Eliot (1928, xvi). On Pound's aesthetics and the "Chineseness" of his translations, see Kern (1996, 181) and Hayot (2003, 21).

1. "Taking Leave of a Friend," Ezra Pound

Pound (2020, 50). For more on Pound's use of such fake or "concocted" calques and for his knowledge of Old English, see my commentary on his translation of "The Seafarer" in Pound (2020, 200–3). See also Xie (1999, 170). Wordsworth (1807, 2:49–50).

As far as I can tell, the first to compare the *lüshi* 律詩 to the sonnet was the very first European to translate Chinese poetry, the French Jesuit missionary Joseph de Prémare (1666–1736), which I recall from reading his manuscripts in Paris some years

ago, though I failed to note precisely where. (Prémare's "transla-
tions," however, were figurist figments of his imagination.) The
more recent mentions can be found in Hawkes (1989, 86), Cooper
(1973, 93), and McCraw (1992, 231 and *passim*). In his book *The
Chinese Sonnet: Meanings of a Form*, Haft (2000) writes that the
"[European] sonnet has often been compared to the *lüshi*," adding
that "the comparison is almost proverbial in educated circles in
China and perhaps cannot be traced to a single source" (205).
("The Chinese Sonnet" in his title refers to *modern* Chinese
imitations of the European sonnet, where actual influence is
involved, not simply analogy.) The comparison was also made by
one of Fenollosa's Japanese tutors, Mr. Hirai, during a lesson in
1896, as recorded in Fenollosa's notebooks (Beinecke YCAL MSS
43, 99–4220, 59), which may have inspired Pound's disparaging
reference to the Tang dynasty as the "Petrarchan age of Li Po" (i.e.,
Li Bai) as opposed to what he tendentiously characterized as "the
great *verse libre* writers" of the Han dynasty (Pound, 1915, 233).

2. "A Farewell," Herbert Giles

Giles (1898, 70). The most influential formulation of this
poetic ideal of expressing thoughts and emotions "beyond the
words" (*yan wai* 言外) appears in the groundbreaking "Remarks
on Poetry" 詩話 by Ouyang Xiu 歐陽脩 (1007–1072), which
launched a new genre of literary criticism. See the Introduction
and excerpts in Owen (1992, chap. 7, esp. 375–77).

3. 送友人 (Seeing Off a Friend)

Li (1977, 2:837). The case for the influence of Sanskrit prosody
on *jintishi* 近體詩 (recent-style poetry) was established in Mair
and Mei (1991, 375–470). For a review of the scholarship on this
topic, see Klein (2018, chap. 3). The distinction between the
spatial and temporal qualities of parallel and nonparallel couplets
may now be commonplace, but see Kao and Mei (1971, 61) and
also Cheng (2016, 73).

4. Categorical Comparatives, with Wang Li

These categories are drawn from chapter 14 of the original edition of Wang (1958). Of course, they are somewhat arbitrary, and a supplementary note to the revised version in Wang's complete works (edited two decades later) cites two treatises appended to a Qing-dynasty rime dictionary where such categories as *caomu huaguo* 草木花果 (herbs, trees, flowers, fruits) are subdivided even further; see Wang (2005, 17:163–77). Wang himself is quick to point out that the categories may be puzzling to modern readers: *shuang* 霜 (frost), for example, is considered a "celestial phenomenon" whereas *bing* 冰 (ice) is a "geographical feature." The same word can also appear in multiple categories depending on its use, such as *ri* 日, which appears under "celestial phenomenon" when it means "sun" and also under "time" when it means "day," or *jian* 劍 (sword), which could be either an "implement" or a "cultural object." Wang also notes that words from separate categories can be paired if their sense suggests a harmonious opposition, such as *tian* 天 (heaven) and *di* 地 (earth), *xue* 雪 (snow) and *bing* 冰 (ice), and *feng* 風 (wind) and *lang* 浪 (waves); Wang (1958, 166; 2005, 177). For an example of the use of "flowing water parallelism" 流水對, see Qiu and Liu (2014, 101).

5. "Sending Off (a) Friend(s)"

For a good sense of the translation challenges posed by Wang Wei's poem, see the splendid little book that originally inspired this one: Weinberger ([1987] 2016).

6. "Le départ d'un ami," Judith Gautier

This poem was not included in the first edition of Gautier's *Le livre de jade* [The book of jade] (1867), published under the pseudonym Judith Walter, but first appeared in *La Revue de Paris* (1901, 812). It was then revised for the new and expanded edition of *Le livre de jade* (1902, 123–24). The estimated percentage of

huiyi 會意 (associative compound) characters is based on studies
of the ancient analytical lexicon *Shuowen jiezi* 說文解字 (Explain-
ing graphs and analyzing characters), cited in Norman (1988,
267n11). Du Fu plays with the double evocation of the sounds of
horses and of wind in the term *xiao-xiao* 蕭蕭 by combining it with
the same word *ming* 鳴 (cry, sough) in our poem, as if one echoed
the other: "The setting sun shines on the great flags. / The horses
cry, and the wind *soughs*" 落日照大旗，馬鳴風蕭蕭; Du Fu, "Five
Poems on Setting Out for the Frontier: Poem 2" 後出塞五首, in
Du (1979, 1:286). For more on Judith Gautier, see Yu (2007).

7. "Saying Good-Bye to a Friend," Amy Lowell and Florence Ayscough

Ayscough and Lowell (1921, 50). For more on the tricky word
qing 青, see "The Color of Nature and Other Hobbyhorses in Ezra
Pound's Cathay" (Billings 2022) and also Chapter 11, below. On the
primacy of sound over some putatively "ideographic" signification
in Tang poetic aesthetics, see Cai (2015) and also Hung (1952, 9).
I often think of A. C. Graham's analogy for the visual effect that
a character might have in the minds of Chinese readers, which is
to imagine what would be lost by spelling the Greek-derived word
sphinx as *sfinks* — i.e., a little, but not much; Graham (1965, 17).

8. "Adieu," W. J. B. Fletcher

Fletcher (1919, 7). Cao (1792, 44.2:95b). For a comprehensive
(but technical) overview of the modern challenges of pronuncia-
tion and transcription of Middle Chinese, see Branner (1999);
also see his online app, which scans poems for their MC tonal
values: *Yīntōng: Chinese Phonological Database* 音通: 聲韻學數
據庫, http://yintong.info/.

9. "Valedicit amico," Angelo Zottoli

Zottoli (1882, 5:457). For more on the flexibility of word order
in early Latin translations of Chinese texts, see Billings (2004,

15). When the Chinese "butterfly" 蝴蝶 appears, I cannot help but think of George Kennedy's (1951, 1955) reflections on the "monosyllabic myth" of classical Chinese, which I am always careful to avoid.

10. "Geleit," Alfred Forke

Forke (1899, 130).

11. "Taking Leave of a Friend," Obata Shigeyoshi

Obata (1922, 94). Pound (2020, 220).

12. "Je reconduis un ami," Bruno Belpaire

Belpaire (1921, 27–28). The attribution of each of the two lines in the neck couplet separately and respectively to the friend and to the speaker is a conventional assumption; see Chapter 18, below.

13. "Le chanson d'adieu," Jean-Marie Guislain

Guislain and Yau (1925, 79). On poets translating languages they cannot read, with the help of an informant, see Yao (2002, 31).

14. "Farewell to a Friend," Henry Hart

Hart (1931, 12). For Mori's comment, see Pound (2020, 225, 228n4). Li Bai, "Visiting Nanyang's 'White' River, I Climb the Rocks and Am Moved to Write This" 遊南陽白水登石激作 (Li, 1977, 3:917). The second poem by Li Bai is "Remembering Minister Cui Zongzhi's Trip to Nanyang to Present Me with an Ancient Style Zither, I Strum Tearfully and Reminisce" 憶崔郎中宗之游南陽遺吾孔子琴，撫之潸然感舊 (Li, 1977, 2:1082). Wang Zhihuan's famous quatrain is "Mounting the Yellow Crane Pavilion" 登鸛雀樓; *Quan Tangshi* (1792, 253:1a), facsimile at https://ctext.org/library.pl?if=en&file=71291&page=38. The map

is found in Xu (1693, 1, seq. 19); facsimile at https://nrs.lib.harvard
.edu/urn-3:fhcl:12502111?n=19.

Several years ago, I translated a selection of about thirty poems
including several sonnets by the late-Ming philosopher Li Zhi
李贄 (1527–1602)—a contemporary of Shakespeare's, though living
a world away—using an earlier prototype of the format I am now
proposing, in which I separated the couplets but did not use
hemistiches, as can be seen in Li ([1590] 2016). Since then, I've
decided there is more to be gained by indicating and emphasizing
the difference between the parallel and the nonparallel couplets,
using hemistiches for the former but not the latter, despite the
arbitrariness of that distinction. Indeed, sometimes couplets that
ought to be chatty flow toward the parallel, and couplets that ought
to be parallel wander from the straight and narrow. Moreover, the
method works well for pentasyllabics, but heptasyllabics make for
very long lines in English, which cry out for hemistiches through-
out, not just for the parallel couplets. Owen sometimes does this
with heptasyllabic poems; for one example, see Owen (1992, 424).

15. "A Farewell to a Friend," Walter Bynner and Kiang Kang-hu

Bynner and Kiang (1939, 57).

16. "J'ai reconduit mon ami . . . ," Tchou Kia Kien and Armand Gandon)

Tchou and Gandon (1930, 72). Hawkes shared Tchou's
disbelief that Chinese parallelism could ever be gracefully
rendered into a European language: "You might think that if
any single formal feature of Chinese verse must be carried over
into the English translation in order to convey some impression
of the original, it is surely this. Yet any attempt at reproducing
in English the antitheses of Chinese poetry leads at once to
orotundity—diffuse verbosity infinitely removed from the neat
conciseness which is a central quality of Chinese verse. There are

simply too many syllables in English. The ingeniously compressed epigrams and conceits of the original unpack into those flaccid orientalisms so familiar to readers of translations" (Hawkes 1989, 90). All this is true enough of what has been done but not, I believe, of what can be done.

17. "Saying Farewell to a Friend," Robert Payne

Payne (1960, 170). Both the poem from the *Shijing* 詩經 (*Classic of Poetry*, "Chariot Charge" 車攻, Mao #179) and the story from the *Zuozhuan* 左傳 (*Commentary of Zuo*, "Year 18 of Duke Xiang" 襄公十八年) are cited by Li Bai's Qing-dynasty editor Wang Qi, who comments: "As the horses of host and traveler are about to take different paths, they cry out with a long *xiao xiao*, as if they also experienced the feeling of being separated from the herd. If it was like this even for the beasts, how could the men themselves have endured it?" 主客之馬將分道，而蕭蕭長鳴，亦若有離羣之感，畜猶如此，人何以堪 (Li 1977, 2:837).

18. 語譯 (Paraphrase), Xu Zhengzhong

Xu (2004, 140). Pound (2014, 5).

Digression: *Peng* 蓬 vs. *Peng* 篷

The one and only complete copy of the early Southern Song (1127–1279) woodcut edition is conserved in Japan at the Seikadō Bunko 靜嘉堂文庫. (This edition is famous for its variant reading of a line in Li Bai's most famous poem, "Quiet Night Thoughts" 靜夜思: "mountain [and] moon" 山月, instead of "bright moon" 明月.) It is the edition used as the control text for a new comprehensive critical edition of Li Bai's collected works by the Taiwanese scholar Yu Xianhao (2015, 5:2132). Remarkably, the only gloss on this poem that was thought significant enough to be retained when Xiao's edition was later reedited for inclusion in the *Siku quanshu* 四庫全書 (Complete library in four treasuries) was Xiao's gloss on *peng* 蓬 (Li 1792, 18:2a). But among the glosses in Yang's (lost) original edition, he had evidently also noted that *peng* 蓬 occurs in a much earlier poem by Cao Zhi 曹植 (192–232 CE), called *Xujie bian* 吁嗟篇 (Sighing), which is a moving lament about his years of exile from court: "Alas, this rolling tumbleweed—how can it live all alone in the world?" 吁嗟此 轉蓬, 居世何獨然 (Li 1291, 18:1b), facsimile at https://library.ctext .org/h0070175/h0070175_0988.jpg.

　　Bao Zhao 鮑照 (414–466) was one of Li Bai's favorite poets, if the number of allusions to his poetry is any measure. The line appears in Bao's renowned *Wu cheng fu* 蕪城賦 (Rhapsody on the overgrown city), in *Wen xuan* 文選 (Selections of fine literature), edited by Xiao Tong 蕭統, the crown prince of the Liang 梁 dynasty (502–557). The standard editions are Xiao (1986) in Chinese and Knechtges (1982–1996) in English, but I used the searchable text and facsimile of the Chongwen shuju 崇文書局 reprint (1869, 同治八年) of a woodcut edition with a preface dated 嘉慶 十四年 (1809, 11:12a), facsimile at https://ctext.org/library.pl?if =gb&file=94380&page=290. And why not? I mean, what is the internet for? The poem by Wang Sengda 王僧達 (423–458) is "On Antiquity, with the Prince" 和琅邪王依古, also in Xiao (1869, 30:4b), https://ctext.org/library.pl?if=gb&file=94384&page=75.

19. "Farewell to a Friend," Adet Lin

　　Lin (1970, 33).

20. "Taking Leave of a Friend," Innes Herdan

　　Herdan (1973, 231). Yu (2011, 2:993). In his own paraphrase, however, Yu recreates the ambiguity of the original without committing to his maverick reading. He reiterates the idea in his comprehensive critical edition a few years later but also quotes a late-Qing commentary to the contrary, knowing full well the tradition he kicks against: "Thus your traveler's thoughts easily disperse like floating clouds, and my feelings as an old friend are just like the setting sun" (Direct Explanations of Li's Poetry [1775]) 故爾遊子之意, 若浮雲而易散; 我故人之情, 當落日而倍切. 《李詩直解》 (Yu, 2015, 5:2136).

21. "Farewell to a Friend," Xu Yuanchong

Xu (2012, preface).

22. "taking leaves (1)," "parting friend," Harry Gilonis

Gilonis (2010, F.1, F.5). Housman (1917, 57). Pope (1713, 2).

23. Tonal Balance: *Ping* 平 ☺ and *Ze* 仄 ☻

Even this description of the metrical rules and permutations for the Chinese sonnet are simplified. For a more detailed description, along with a next-level introduction to the *lüshi*, see Ashmore (2008, 169–72).

24. "Seeing Off a Friend," Jonathan Stalling

Stalling (2013). Schleiermacher (2012, 49). For a detailed introduction to Stalling's interlingual experiments with the *jueju* 絕句 (quatrain), see Billings (2021).

25. "Seeing Off a Friend," Gregory Whincup

Whincup (1987, 30).

26. "Seeing Off a Friend," Edward Chang

Chang (2007, 62).

27. "Seeing Off a Friend," Red Pine / Bill Porter

Porter (2003, 101).

28. Yinsong: In Song

Xu (2015, 41). For another translation of this famous passage in the *Book of Documents* 書經, see Owen (1992, 26). On phonoaesthemes in Chinese poetry, see the eye-opening work of Smith (2015).

29. "Seeing Off a Friend," Timothy Billings

The various texts of Liu Xie make consistent citations challenging, but see Liu (2008, chap. 35 麗辭, 253, 258) and also Shih's English edition (1959, 190, 194). On rhyming, see Shih (1959, 189) and Liu (1919, chap. 34 章句, 7:7b). See Kao and Mei (1971, 61, 131, 64) and also Kao and Mei (1978). Nida (2012, 128). For a beautifully nuanced reading of "In a Station of the Metro," which opens onto an insightful reflection on the contradictions in modernist European assumptions about Chinese writing and the nature of the image, see Bush (2012, chap. 1, 30–71). See Yip (1969, 21, 212) and also Yip (1997, 180). Watson (1971, 147). Boodberg (1955, 19). On "poetry chats" 詩話, see the notes to Chapter 2. The heptasyllabic line is from a famous quatrain called "Night Mooring at Maple Bridge" 楓橋夜泊, by Li Bai's contemporary Zhang Ji 張繼 (715?–779).

Epilogue: What's in a Name? The Sonnet

For his "Pace non trovo, et non ò da far guerra" (cxxxiv), see Petrarca (1964, 186). On the influence of Sanskrit on Chinese prosody, see notes to Chapter 3.

The "Eight Defects" 八病 are as follows:

1) *Pingtou* 平頭 (flat head) occurs when characters #1 and #2 in both lines of the first couplet have the same tone, in particular (according to some) if they are both "flat," i.e., level tones.

2) *Shangwei* 上尾 (rising tail) occurs when character #5 in both lines of a couplet have the same tone (except, of course, when they intentionally rhyme).

3) *Fengyao* 蜂腰 (wasp waist) occurs when the middle of a line feels tiny because characters #2 and #4 have the same tone or because characters #2 and #5 both have voiced initials and character #3 has a voiceless initial.

4) *Hexi* 鶴膝 (crane knees) occurs when the last character in both the first line and the fifth line are the same.

5) *Dayun* 大韻 (big rhyme) occurs when a character anywhere else within a couplet rhymes with its end rhyme.

6) *Xiaoyun* 小韻 (little rhyme) occurs when any two characters within a couplet rhyme with each other.

7) *Pangniu* 旁紐 (sidewise tie) occurs when two characters in a couplet have the same initial, unless they are part of a compound.

8) *Zhengniu* 正紐 (straight tie) occurs when two characters in a couplet have the same final, even though they have different tones.

See the entry on *babing* 八病 in *Handian* 漢典, https://www.zdic.net/hant/八病. For a short summary of the "Eight Faults" in English, see Watson (1971, 111). For an introduction to Shakespeare's prosody, see Ramsey (1979, chap. 4). For his famous comment on "The Verse" in the second edition of *Paradise Lost* (1668), see Milton (1957, 210). Cheng (2016, 75–77).

Credits

Xu, Yuanchong 許淵沖. *300 Tang Poems*. Classical Chinese Poetry and Prose Series. English ed. Beijing: China Intercontinental Press, 2012.

Xu, Zhengzhong 許正中. *Tangdai lüshi xinshang* 唐代律詩欣賞 [Appreciating Tang-dynasty regulated verse]. Taibei: Dongda tushu gongsi, 2004.

References

Ashmore, Robert. 2008. "Recent-Style *Shi* Poetry: Pentasyllabic Regulated Verse (*Wuyan Lüshi*)." In *How to Read Chinese Poetry: A Guided Anthology*, ed. Cai Zong-qi, 161–80. New York: Columbia University Press.

Ayscough, Florence, and Amy Lowell. 1921. *Fir-Flower Tablets* 松花箋: *Poems Translated from the Chinese*. Boston: Houghton Mifflin.

Belpaire, Bruno. 1921. *Quarante poésies de Li Tai Pé*. Paris: Imprimerie nationale.

Branner, David Prager. 1999. "A Neutral Transcription System for Teaching Medieval Chinese." *T'ang Studies* 17: 1–111.

———. n.d. *Yīntōng: Chinese Phonological Database* 音通: 聲韻學數據庫. http://yintong.info/.

Billings, Timothy. 2004. "Jesuit Fish in Chinese Nets: Athanasius Kircher and the Translation of the Nestorian Tablet." *Representations* 87 (Summer): 1–42.

———. 2021. "The English Jueju: Jonathan Stalling's Sino-English Poetics in an American Context." In *Yingelishi: Jonathan Stalling's Interlanguage Art*, ed. Chen Wang, 168–85. Hong Kong: University of Hong Kong Museum and Art Gallery.

———. 2022. "The Color of Nature and Other Hobbyhorses in Ezra Pound's Cathay." *Make It New: The Ezra Pound Society Journal* 6, no. 3 (Spring). https://makeitnew.ezrapoundsociety .org/en/volume-vi/6-3-may-2022/essay-vi-3.

Boodberg, Peter. 1955. "Cedules from a Berkeley Workshop in Asiatic Philology (with a Postscript by S. H. Chen)." Berkeley, CA: Self-published.

Bush, Christopher. 2012. *Ideographic Modernism: China, Writing, Media*. Oxford: Oxford University Press.

Bynner, Witter, and Kiang Kang-hu 江亢虎. (1929) 1939. *The Jade Mountain: A Chinese Anthology*. New York: Knopf.

Cai, Zong-qi. 2015. "Sound over Ideograph: The Basis of Chinese Poetic Art." *Journal of Chinese Literature and Culture* 2, no. 2 (November): 545–72.

Cao, Xuequan 曹學佺. 1792. *Shicang lidai shixuan* 石倉歷代詩選 [The stone repository selection of poetry from all ages]. In *Siku quanshu* 四庫全書 [Complete library in four treasuries], 1387–94. https://ctext.org/library.pl?if=en&res=6177.

Chang, Edward C. 2007. *How to Read a Chinese Poem: A Bilingual Anthology of Tang Poetry*. BookSurge [CreateSpace] Publishing.

Cheng, François 程抱一. (1977) 2016. *Chinese Poetic Writing: With an Anthology of Tang Poetry*. Trans. Donald A. Riggs and Jerome Seaton. Expanded ed. Hong Kong and New York: The Chinese University of Hong Kong and New York Review of Books.

Cooper, Arthur. 1973. *Li Po and Tu Fu*. Harmondsworth: Penguin.

Ctext.org. *Zhongguo zhexueshu dianzihua jihua* 中國哲學書電子 化計劃 [Chinese philosophical texts digitization project]. Ed. Douglas Sturgeon. http:www.ctext.org.

Du, Fu. 1979. *Du Fu shi xiangzhu* 杜甫詩詳註 [Detailed annotations on Du Fu's poetry]. Ed. Qiu Zhaoao 仇兆鰲. 5 vols. Beijing: Zhonghua shuju.

Eliot, Thomas Stearns. 1928. "Introduction." In Ezra Pound, *Selected Poetry*, vii–xxv. Faber & Gwyer.

Fang, Achilles. 1955. "From Imagism to Whitmanism in Recent Chinese Poetry: A Search for a Poetics That Failed." In *Indiana*

University Conference on Oriental-Western Literary Relations,
      ed. Horst Franz and G. L. Anderson, 177–89. Chapel Hill:
      University of North Carolina Press.

Fletcher, William John Bainbrigge. 1919. *More Gems of Chinese*
      Poetry, Translated into English Verse. With Comparative
      Passages from English Literature / 英譯唐詩選續集. Shanghai:
      Commercial Press Ltd.

Forke, Alfred. 1899. *Blüthen Chinesischer Dichtung* [Flowers of
      Chinese poetry]. Magdeburg: Commissionsverlag, Faber'sche
      Buchdruckerei, A & R Faber.

Gautier, Judith. 1901. "Poèmes chinois de tous les temps. *La*
      Revue de Paris (June): 805–20.

——. 1902. *Le livre de jade* / 玉書: *Poésies traduites du chinois.*
      Nouvelle édition considérablement augmenté. Paris: Félix
      Juven.

Gautier (Walter), Judith. 1867. *Le livre de jade* / 白玉詩書. Paris:
      Alphonse Lemerre.

Giles, Herbert. 1898. *Chinese Poetry in English Verse.* London:
      B. Quaritch.

Gilonis, Harry. 2010. *eye-blink.* London: Veer.

Graham, A. C. 1965. *Poems of the Late Tang.* Harmondsworth:
      Penguin.

Guislain, Jean–Marie, and Yau Chang-Foo 姚昌復. 1925. *La*
      cigale éperdue: Une transcription de Li-Taï-Peh. D'après les
      caractères traduits et commentés par Yau Chang-Foo [The
      lost cicada: A transcription of Li Taibai. After the characters
      translated with commentary by Yao Changfu]. Paris: Albert
      Messein.

Haft, Lloyd L. 2000. *The Chinese Sonnet: Meanings of a Form.*
      Leiden: Research School CNWS.

Hart, Henry. 1931. *A Chinese Market: Lyrics from the Chinese in*
      English Verse. Peking: The French Bookstore.

Hawkes, David. 1989. "Chinese Poetry and the English Reader."
      In *Classical, Modern, and Humane: Essays in Chinese Litera-*
      ture, ed. John Minford and Siu-kit Wong, 79–99. Hong Kong:
      The Chinese University Press.

Hayot, Eric. 2003. *Chinese Dreams: Pound, Brecht, Tel Quel.* Ann Arbor: University of Michigan Press.

Herdan, Innes. 1973. *The Three Hundred T'ang Poems.* Taipei: Far East Book Co.

Housman, Alfred Edward. (1896) 1917. *A Shropshire Lad.* New York: John Lane.

Hung, William 洪業. 1952. *Tu Fu: China's Greatest Poet.* Cambridge, MA: Harvard University Press.

Kao Yu-kung 高友工 and Mei Tsu-lin 梅祖麟. 1971. "Syntax, Diction, and Imagery in T'ang Poetry." *Harvard Journal of Asiatic Studies* 31: 49–136.

———. 1978. "Meaning, Metaphor, and Allusion in T'ang Poetry." *Harvard Journal of Asiatic Studies* 38: 281–356.

Kennedy, George A. 1951. "The Monosyllabic Myth." In *Journal of the American Oriental Society* 71, no. 3 (July–September): 161–66. Reprinted in *Selected Works of George A. Kennedy*, ed. Tien-yi Li, 104–18. New Haven, CT: Yale University Press, 1964.

———. 1955. "The Butterfly Case." *Wenti Papers* 8: 1–47. Reprinted in *Selected Works of George A. Kennedy*, ed. Tien-yi Li, 274–322. New Haven, CT: Yale University Press, 1964.

Kern, Robert. 1996. *Orientalism, Modernism, and the American Poem.* New York: Press Syndicate of the University of Cambridge.

Klein, Lucas. 2018. *The Organization of Distance: Poetry, Translation, Chineseness.* Leiden: Brill.

Mair, Victor H., and Mei Tsu-Lin 梅祖麟. 1991. "The Sanskrit Origins of Recent Style Prosody." *Harvard Journal of Asiatic Studies* 51, no. 2 (December): 375–470.

McCraw, David R. 1992. *Du Fu's Laments from the South.* Honolulu: University of Hawai'i Press.

Milton, John. (1668) 1957. *John Milton: Complete Poems and Major Prose.* Ed. Merritt Hughes. New York: Macmillan.

Li, Bai 李白. 1291 (至元辛卯). *Fenlei buzhu Li Taibai shi* 分類補註李太白詩 [Categorized with supplemental annotations, Li Taibai's poetry]. Ed. Xiao Shiyun 蕭士贇 and Yang Qixian 楊齊賢. 25 vols. https://ctext.org/library.pl?if=en&res=96003.

———. 1792. *Li Taibai ji fenlei buzhu* 《李太白集分類補註》
[The collected Li Bai, categorized with supplemental
annotations]. Ed. Xiao Shiyun 蕭士贇 and Yang Qixian 楊齊
賢. 30 vols. In *Siku quanshu* 四庫全書 [Complete library in
four treasuries]. Beijing. https://ctext.org/library.pl?if=gb&res
=5523.

———. 1977. *Li Taibo quanji* 李太白全集 [The complete
collected Li Bai]. Ed. Wang Qi 王琦 and the Zhonghua
Shuju Bianjibu 中華書局編輯部 [China Book Company
editorial division]. 3 vols. Beijing: Zhonghua shuju.

Li, Zhi 李贄. (1590, 1599) 2016. "Selected Poems," trans. Timothy
Billings and Yan Zinan 顏子楠. In *A Book to Burn and a Book
to Keep (Hidden): Selected Writings*, ed. Rivi Handler-Spitz,
Pauline Lee, and Haun Saussy, 211–29, 295–316. Translations
from the Asian Classics Series. New York: Columbia University
Press.

Liu, Wan. 1988. "Classical Poetry in China and England: A
Comparison of Formal Stylistics." *Comparative Literature
Studies* 25, no. 2: 152–66.

Liu, Xie 劉勰. (6th c.) 1919. *Wenxin diaolong* 文心雕龍
[The literary mind and the carving of dragons]. Ed. Zhang, Yuanji
張元濟. In *Sibu congkan chubian* 四部叢刊初編. https://ctext
.org/library.pl?if=gb&res=77660.

Liu, Xie 劉勰. 1959. *The Literary Mind and the Carving of
Dragons: A Study of Thought and Pattern in Chinese Litera-
ture*. Trans. Vincent Yu-chung Shih. New York: Columbia
University Press.

Liu, Xie 劉勰. 2008. Wenxin diaolong *jiedu* 《文心雕龙》解读
[The literary mind and the carving of dragons Interpreted].
Ed. Yuan, Jixi 袁济喜 and Chen, Jiannong 陈建农. Beijing:
Zhongguo Renmin Daxue chubanshe.

Lin, Adet 林如斯. 1970. *Flower Shadows: 40 Poems from the Tang
Dynasty*. 唐詩選譯. Taibei: Taiwan Zhonghua shuju.

Nida, Eugene. (1964) 2012. "Principles of Correspondence." In
The Translation Studies Reader, ed. Lawrence Venuti, 126–40.
New York: Routledge.

Norman, Jerry. 1988. *Chinese*. Cambridge Language Series. Cambridge University Press.

Obata, Shigeyoshi. 1922. *The Works of Li Po, the Chinese Poet*. New York: Dutton.

Owen, Stephen. 1992. *Readings in Chinese Literary Thought*. Cambridge, MA: Council on East Asian Studies, Harvard University.

Payne, Robert. (1947) 1960. *The White Pony: An Anthology of Chinese Poetry*. New York: Mentor.

Petrarca, Francesco (Petrarch). (14th c.) 1964. *"Il Canzoniere" di Francesco Petrarca*. Ed. Gianfranco Contini. Torino: Einaudi.

Pope, Alexander. 1713. *Windsor-Forest*. London: Bernard Lintott.

Pound, Ezra. (1915) 2020. *Cathay: A Critical Edition*. Ed. Timothy Billings. Introduction by Christopher Bush. Foreword by Haun Saussy. New York: Fordham University Press.

Pound, Ezra. (1928) 2014. *Pound's "Cavalcanti": An Edition of the Translation, Notes, and Essays*. Ed. David Anderson. Princeton, NJ: Princeton University Press.

Pine, Red (William Porter). 2003. *Poems of the Masters: China's Classic Anthology of T'ang and Sung Dynasty Verse*. Port Townsend, WA: Copper Canyon.

Qiu, Xieyou 邱燮友 and Liu Zhenghao 劉正浩. 2014. *Xinyi Qianjiashi* 新譯千家詩 [Newly interpreted poems of the thousand masters]. Taibei: Sanmin shuju, 2014.

Quan Tangshi 全唐詩 [Complete Tang poetry]. 1792. In *Siku quanshu* 四庫全書 [Complete library in four treasuries]. https://ctext.org/library.pl?if=en&res=6484.

Ramsey, Paul. 1979. *The Fickle Glass: A Study of Shakespeare's Sonnets*. New York: AMS Press.

Schleiermacher, Friedrich. (1813) 2012. "On the Different Methods of Translating." Trans. Susan Bernofsky. In *The Translation Studies Reader*, ed. Lawrence Venuti, 43–63. New York: Routledge.

Smith, Jonathan. 2015. "Sound Symbolism in the Reduplicative Vocabulary of the *Shijing*." *Journal of Chinese Literature and Culture* 2, no. 2 (November): 258–85.

Stalling, Jonathan. 2013. "Evolving from Embryo and Changing the Bones: Translating the Sonorous (夺胎換骨：译诗存音)." *Cha: An Asian Literary Journal* 22 (December), https://www.asiancha.com/content/view/1621/421/.

Tchou Kia Kien 朱家煜 and Armand Gandon. (1927) 1930. *Ombres de fleurs* [Flower shadows]. Beijing: Albert Nachbaur.

Wang, Li 王力. 1958. *Hanyu shilü xue* 漢語詩律學 [Studies in Chinese versification]. Shanghai: Shanghai Jiaoyu Chubanshe.

———. 2005. *Wang Li Quanji* 王力全集. Beijing: Zhonghua shuju.

Watson, Burton. 1971. *Chinese Lyricism: Shih Poetry from the Second to the Twelfth Century*. New York: Columbia University Press.

Weinberger, Eliot. (1987) 2016. *Nineteen Ways of Looking at Wang Wei (with More Ways)*. New York: New Directions.

Whincup, Gregory. 1987. *The Heart of Chinese Poetry*. New York: Anchor.

Wordsworth, William. 1807. *Poems*. Vol. 2, 49–50. London: Longman, Hurst, Rees, & Orme.

Yan, Zinan 顏子楠. 2018. "Luoji de qizhong leixing: Songdai jintishi de jiegou zhuyi" 邏輯的七種類型：宋代近體詩的結構主義批評 [Seven types of logic: a structuralist critique of Song-dynasty recent-style poetry]. *Xin Songxue* 新宋學 [New Song studies] 7: 97–135.

Yao, Steven. 2002. *Translation and the Languages of Modernism*. New York: Palgrave Macmillan.

Yu, Pauline. 2007. "'Your Alabaster in This Porcelain': Judith Gautier's *Le Livre de jade*." *PMLA* 122, no. 2: 464–82.

Xie, Ming. *Ezra Pound and the Appropriation of Chinese Poetry: "Cathay," Translation, and Imagism*. New York: Garland, 1999.

Xiao, Tong 蕭統. *Wen Xuan or Selections of Refined Literature*. Trans. David R. Knechtges. 3 vols. Princeton, NJ: Princeton University Press, 1982–1996.

Xiao, Tong 蕭統 and Li Shan 李善. (6th c.) 1986. *Wen xuan* 文選 [Selections of fine literature]. Shanghai: Shanghai guji chubanshe.

Xiao, Tong 蕭統, Li Shan 李善, and Chun Xi 淳熙. 1869. *Wen xuan Li Shan zhu liushi juan* 文選李善注六十卷 [Selections of fine literature, annotated by Li Shan, in sixty volumes]. Hubei: Chongwen shuju. https://ctext.org/library.pl?if=gb&res=81549.

Xu, Jianshun 徐健順. 2015. *Wo ai yinsong* 我爱吟诵 [I love chanting poetry]. 3rd ed. Guilin: Guangxi shifan daxue chubanshe.

Xu Yongzhi 許永芝. 1693. *Nanyang xian zhi* 南陽縣志 [Nanyang county gazetteer]. 6 vols. https://nrs.lib.harvard.edu/urn-3:fhcl:12502111.

Xu, Yuanchong 許淵沖. 2012. *300 Tang Poems*. English ed. Classical Chinese Poetry and Prose Series. Beijing: China Intercontinental Press.

Xu, Zhengzhong 許正中. 2004. *Tangdai lüshi xinshang* 唐代律詩欣賞 [Appreciating Tang-dynasty regulated verse]. Taibei: Dongda tushu gongsi.

Yip, Wai-lim. 1969. *Ezra Pound's Cathay*. Princeton, NJ: Princeton University Press.

———. (1976) 1997. *Chinese Poetry: An Anthology of Major Modes and Genres*. Durham, NC: Duke University Press.

Yu, Xianhao 郁賢浩. 2011. *Xinyi Libai shi quanji* 新譯李白詩全集 [New readings of Li Bai's complete collected poetry]. 3 vols. Taibei: Sanmin shuju.

———. 2015. *Li Taibai quanji jiaozhu* 李太白全集校注 [Li Taibai's complete works: a critical edition]. 8 vols. Nanjing: Fenghuang chubanshe.

Young, David. 1990. *Five T'ang Poets: Wang Wei, Li Po, Tu Fu, Li Ho, Li Shang-yin*. Oberlin, OH: Oberlin College Press.

Zottoli, Angelo. 1878–1882. *Cursus Litteraturae Sinicae* [The course of Chinese literature]. 5 vols. Shanghai: Tou-se-we.

TIMOTHY BILLINGS is Professor of English and Comparative Literature at Middlebury College, where his expertise spans classical Chinese literature and Shakespeare. Billings has edited and translated three award-winning bilingual critical editions that draw upon Chinese sources: Victor Segalen's *Stèles* / 古今碑錄 (with Christopher Bush), Matteo Ricci's *Essay on Friendship* / 交友論: *One Hundred Maxims for a Chinese Prince*, and Ezra Pound's *Cathay* / 耀. His work bridges the gap between Eastern and Western literary traditions and enriches the study and appreciation of classical Chinese poetry and its influence on global literature.

Printed in the USA
CPSIA information can be obtained
at www.ICGtesting.com
JSHW012114251024
72428JS00001B/1/J

9 781531 508357